THE ARCHITECTURE OF SUNDERLAND 1700-1914

THE ARCHITECTURE OF SUNDERLAND 1700-1914

MICHAEL JOHNSON
& GRAHAM POTTS

The
History
Press

First published 2013

The History Press
The Mill, Brimscombe Port
Stroud, Gloucestershire, GL5 2QG
www.thehistorypress.co.uk

British Library Cataloguing in Publication Data.
A catalogue record for this book is available from the British Library.

ISBN 978 0 7524 9923 9

Typesetting and origination by The History Press
Printed in Great Britain

Contents

Acknowledgements

This book is based on research carried out as part of the England's Past For Everyone project, funded by the Heritage Lottery Fund in co-operation with the Universities of London, Durham and Sunderland and the Durham Victoria County History Trust (www.victoriacountyhistory.ac.uk/counties/durham).

The authors would like to thank the following EPE and VCH staff for their assistance during the production of this volume:

Matthew Bristow – Historic Environment Research Manager
Gill Cookson – County Editor, Durham Victoria County History
Alan Thacker – Consultant Editor, Victoria County History
Elizabeth Williamson – Executive Editor, Victoria County History

All photographs are by Michael Johnson unless otherwise noted.

Introduction

Sunderland is a city of ancient origin, but its modern form is largely a product of the eighteenth and nineteenth centuries, when coalmining and shipbuilding fuelled rapid expansion and development. This book examines Sunderland's architectural history during the highpoint of its growth and prosperity. The elegant buildings of the Georgian period became vital components of the town's developing infrastructure. The Victorian period imbued Sunderland with new churches and chapels, as well as a diverse range of public and commercial buildings. Finally, the exuberant buildings of the Edwardian period represent the pinnacle of Sunderland's architectural achievement. Exploring these structures in depth, this book also examines the major architectural practices that contributed to the formation of Sunderland's built environment.

Outwardly Sunderland is an ordinary provincial city with no great claim to significance. Its architecture largely conforms to national patterns in terms of styles, building materials and construction methods. However, the city exhibits many achievements and local curiosities that are worthy of note. Its townscape is studded with buildings of architectural and historical interest, from the classical church of Holy Trinity to the spectacular mansions of Victorian industrialists [Fig 1]. St Andrew's Church at Roker is a building of national significance, a magnificent Arts and Crafts church featuring designs by William Morris and Sir Edward Burne-Jones. Further down the social hierarchy, Sunderland developed a distinctive form of workers' housing known as Sunderland cottages, which are virtually unique in England. Placing these buildings in their historical context, the book explores the economic, social and cultural forces that shaped Sunderland's architecture and landscape.

A number of important studies of Sunderland's development have been published in recent years. Most significantly, the Victoria County History produced two valuable books, *Sunderland and Its Origins: Monks to Mariners* by Maureen M. Meikle and Christine M. Newman (2008) and *Sunderland: Building a City* by Gill Cookson (2010). These provide a comprehensive analysis of Sunderland's historical development and its urban form, but discussion of the city's architecture is by necessity limited. The current study attempts to locate Sunderland's architectural history in the context of the national mainstream, revealing how the major trends and debates within British architecture influenced the townscape. Discussion focuses on the buildings erected within the old Borough of Sunderland during the period 1700–1914. These chronological parameters encompass a time of remarkable prosperity and expansion. The creation of Sunderland parish in 1719 coincided with an economic boom and the building of new streets and houses. At the end of our period, the catastrophe of the First World War provides an appropriate stopping point. Much of Sunderland's architectural heritage has already been lost to developers, and for this reason the book uses archival documents and images to reconstruct its vanishing townscapes. In the text, ★ denotes a building that has been demolished.

Modern Sunderland did not develop from one central nucleus, but from three smaller settlements clustered around the mouth of the River Wear [Plate 1]. The oldest was Monkwearmouth, a monastic settlement on the north bank. South of the river and further inland, Bishopwearmouth belonged (as its name suggests) to the Bishops of Durham. To the east lay the 'sundered land', so called because it was divided from the lands of the Wearmouth monks by the river. This area was designated Sunderland parish in 1719, and the township began to spread along the line of High Street, eventually fusing with the older parish of Bishopwearmouth. The building of the Wearmouth Bridge in 1796 joined these areas with the ancient parish of Monkwearmouth to the north. From this point on Sunderland was increasingly recognised as a single town, and the three parishes were officially incorporated in 1835.

During this period Sunderland's prosperity was largely based on coal. Beginning in the seventeenth century, coal from across the Durham coalfield was transported down the river in flat-bottomed keels before being transferred into collier brigs and shipped down the coast. From 1815 new railways and wagonways facilitated this process. Wearmouth Colliery, at one time the deepest in the world, began producing in 1835, and the South Docks were built in 1850 to allow ever greater quantities of coal to be shipped. Ancillary industries developed in response to this burgeoning trade: lime-burning, salt-making, pottery-making and glass-making all flourished thanks to the steady supply of cheap coal. A notable success was James Hartley's Glassworks, located above the Lambton and Hetton coal-drops near Galley's Gill. Glass was Sunderland's leading export after coal and salt, and by 1850 Hartley was producing a third of all plate glass made in Britain.[1]

Sunderland's other great industry was of course shipbuilding. This was first recorded in Hendon in 1346, and the industry was well established by 1717 when the River Wear Commission was founded. The Commissioners dredged the river and made a series of improvements to the town's infrastructure. Private companies built a South Pier (1726–59) and North Pier (1788–1802), as well as the North Dock (1837), Hudson Dock (1850) and Hendon Dock (1868). These were significant feats of engineering which transformed Sunderland's commercial prospects. During the nineteenth century shipbuilding became Sunderland's dominant industry, employing 20 per cent of the town's workforce. Scores of shipyards lined the river banks, initially occupied with the construction of wooden vessels. Adapting to new technologies, the town's first iron ship was built in 1852 and steel ships were being produced by 1882. Shipbuilding was key to the town's identity and a major source of pride to workers and their families. Indeed, nineteenth-century Sunderland regarded itself as the largest shipbuilding town in the world.

Industry left its scars on the landscape and cast a black pall across the sky, but it also fuelled much of the architectural development that Sunderland experienced from the seventeenth century onwards. Coal-fitters and ship-owners erected fine houses for their own occupation, as well as churches and other amenities for the working populace.[2] As the town became industrialised, the affluent middle class moved to superior terraced housing on the Fawcett Estate. However, the opening of Wearmouth Bridge in 1796 transformed Fawcett Street into Sunderland's major north-south axis, and by 1850 it was developing into a commercial rather than a residential street. The wealthiest citizens moved to the suburbs beyond Mowbray Park, many building private villas in fashionable architectural styles. The working classes lived in terraces built around sites of industry, many of them in the distinctive single-storey terraces known as Sunderland cottages.

Industrial activity stimulated massive population growth. At the start of the nineteenth century Sunderland's population stood at 26,511. By the end of the century it had soared to 182,260.[3] With the town growing in scale and complexity, effective administration became a pressing need. Unfortunately, Sunderland's local government was characterised by conflict and confusion for much of the period under study. In 1851, however, the Sunderland Borough Act greatly clarified this situation, abolishing all commissioners except the River Wear Commissioners and giving their powers to the Corporation. An Improvement Act was passed in 1867, enabling the Corporation to tackle unsanitary areas, and a new Improvement Committee was established under the leadership of Alderman James Williams.

Prosperity engendered civic pride, and this was manifested in a wave of new buildings. Sunderland's elite citizens endowed the town with private villas, speculative housing and much-needed public amenities, including museums, libraries, schools, hospitals, public parks and a Town Hall. These were vital components of any ambitious town. Throughout this tumultuous development Sunderland's architecture broadly followed the patterns observed in other provincial towns and cities. During the nineteenth century Britain became the richest and most powerful country in the world, but Victorian architecture was dominated by the influence of the past. The major stylistic movements of the period were Neoclassicism and the Gothic Revival. Neoclassicism was based on the architecture of Ancient Greece and Rome; it strove for harmony and perfection in its use of symmetry and exact mathematical proportions. The Gothic Revival aimed to resurrect the architecture and the fabled spirituality of the Middle Ages. The style was inspired by nature – conceived as God's creation – and for this reason it was mainly used for religious buildings. The hallmark of the Gothic style is the pointed arch. Ribbed vaults, sculpted foliage and sinuous tracery derived from plant forms are also characteristic. These styles were used alongside each other, and became locked in a bitter rivalry known as the Battle of the Styles.

Neoclassicism dominated eighteenth- and early nineteenth-century architecture in the North East. In the 1830s, for example, the neighbouring town of Newcastle was transformed by the speculative builder Richard Grainger (1797–1861), who used the talents of architects like John Dobson (1787–1865), John and Benjamin Green, and Walker and Wardle to lay out stately classical streets. Sunderland made a number of attempts to emulate the classical townscapes of Newcastle, without much success, but here too classicism was the dominant idiom until the mid-nineteenth century. Holy Trinity Church (1719), the Exchange Building (1814), the *Athenaeum (1839) and terraced housing on the Fawcett Estate (*c*.1820–45) all display elements of classicism. In the field of ecclesiastical architecture, classicism was eventually supplanted by the Gothic style. Sunderland's first Gothic Revival building was *St Thomas's Church (1829), and a wave of neo-medieval churches followed, their soaring spires forming prominent elements in the townscape. The power of the Gothic Revival was such that it extended beyond the religious sphere and was used for building types that had no medieval precedents, including railway stations and office buildings.

The Industrial Revolution transformed Britain during this period and had many positive effects, but it also spawned such evils as pollution, slum housing and child labour. The Arts and Crafts movement was a reaction against the horrors of industry, and in particular its impact upon the decorative arts. The leader of the movement was William Morris (1834–96), a writer, designer and social reformer. In his view, machine-made goods were inferior to handcrafted products and machine production reduced the worker to a slave, crushing all possibility of artistic expression. A Libertarian Socialist, Morris wished to create a society that valued the worker and simple, honest craftsmanship. Very soon Morris gathered a following among young designers; this was the basis of the Arts and Crafts movement. A central principle of their work was truth to materials: advocates used materials in ways that were appropriate to their properties and which celebrated their variety, colour and texture. Sunderland is fortunate to possess one of the finest expressions of Arts and Crafts architecture in Britain, St Andrew's Church at Roker (1907). In the domestic sphere, Langham Tower (1886–91) is a Victorian mansion inspired by Norman Shaw's groundbreaking designs for Cragside in

Northumberland. The local architect C.A. Clayton Greene (1874–1949) designed a number of buildings in an Arts and Crafts idiom, including St Gabriel's Church (1912) and Hammerton Hall (1914). These buildings survive as highlights in the sprawling townscape, while the surrounding infrastructure serves to illuminate the major patterns of provincial building in the eighteenth and nineteenth centuries. Viewed from a national perspective, Sunderland's architecture may not be distinctive, but it arose from a fascinating local context and was shaped by the town's economic growth and by its people.

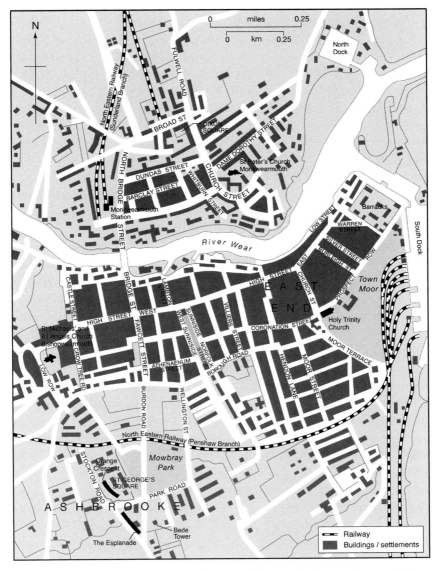

1 Sunderland, *c*.1860, showing the principal streets and features of the town. (By permission of the VCH Executive Editor. Copyright University of London: Cath D'Alton)

Early Development

In the eighteenth century three local Acts of Parliament were passed which were to have a significant effect on the growth and development of Sunderland. In 1717 the River Wear Commissioners were established to bring order to trade on the river, and to provide a framework for developing the economic opportunities of the port. In 1719 the parish of Sunderland was created. This began the Church of England's efforts to cope with the pressures presented by the expanding town, and gave the new parish some organs of local government. Finally, in 1792 an act permitting the building of Wearmouth Bridge made it possible to view the town as a single entity rather than a collection of parishes. If we add the Improvement Act of 1809, which provided the beginnings of a local government structure for the whole township, then Sunderland had gained a framework that would underpin the growth of the town in the subsequent century. All of these acts had implications for building and the design of the townscape, but the one that had the most immediate impact was the creation of Holy Trinity parish.

Origins of a Township

Holy Trinity Church was built at the outset of the Georgian period (1714–1830), an age of elegance and grace in English architecture. The church was designed in the classical style as if to mark the new parish as quite distinct from Bishopwearmouth. The design was radically different from the medieval Gothic of St Michael's Church, and the use of brick contrasted with the stone of Sunderland's two older churches. It was also intended as an auditory church, where the congregation would listen to a charismatic preacher, in contrast to the ritual churches that were built to follow Catholic liturgy. Holy Trinity was a bright, modern church for a new age of prosperity and progress [Plate 2].

The design is attributed to William Etty of York (c.1675–1734) on the basis that he was paid for 'admeasurements in the body of the church'. This has been disputed by some commentators, and the reference may simply indicate that Etty was working as a joiner on woodwork within the building.[4]

However, Etty was also an architect who worked with Sir John Vanbrugh, Colen Campbell and Nicholas Hawksmoor during his career, and he designed a church in Leeds, which coincidentally was also called Holy Trinity (1722–27). He would therefore have been capable of designing a classical church.[5] Externally the church is a modest symmetrical design with a tower at the extreme end of the nave. The whole is executed in red brick made of clay dug from the Town Moor. Dressings of sandstone impart a sense of dignity to the frontage. Tuscan pilasters are clasped to the façade and the large central door is set within a heavily rusticated arch. The tower is a square structure that originally terminated with a cupola, but now only the four pinnacles at the corners remain. Rusticated dressings strengthen the tower itself. The original short chancel still projects at the rear, but a circular apse was added by Rector Daniel Newcome in 1735.

The exterior is modest, but the interior is a revelation. Internally there are no shadowed enclaves or 'dim religious light', but rather a simple rectangular space suffused with light from clear glass windows [Fig 3]. The rectilinear nave is divided by Corinthian columns that support a rich entablature. Each column rests upon a panelled wooden plinth. These originally rose from an expanse of wooden box pews, but the pews were replaced by fine benches in 1935, made using the original oak.[6] At the west end of the nave is a gallery supported on slender Corinthian columns of extremely fine workmanship.[7] The new church also functioned as a seat of local government, and the gallery makes a display of its political loyalties: the arms of George I are flanked by those of the bishops of Durham and London. This was intended to show the parish's loyalty to the Hanoverian succession and indicate that it would give no support to either the Catholic Stuarts or to the republicanism of some Nonconformists. At the east end a low communion rail of turned balusters extends across the breadth of the church. A charming feature is the bow-shaped gate that swings open to allow access to the altar. The pulpit is now situated to one side of the nave but originally stood in front of the altar, where it asserted the primacy of the Word over ritual.

Above the altar, the chancel arch is enriched to form an elaborate Baroque reredos reminiscent of the work of Wren and Hawksmoor. Paired Corinthian columns support a round arch with winged cherubs' heads beaming down from its summit. Towering above are three broken pediments enclosing sculpted symbols – episcopal mitres and an open Bible. Through the arch is the circular apse, with a tripartite Venetian window filled with Victorian stained-glass. The addition of this vestibule-like apse in 1735 reasserted the spiritual role of the church.

The secular role of the building is illustrated at the west end, where a pilaster separates nave from vestry. The vestry is a large chamber that served as the administrative centre of the new parish. Twenty-four elected officials met around an oak table that still survives *in situ*. Many of the decisions that

shaped early Sunderland were made around this table. The officials involved
in administering the parish are commemorated in stalls at the west end of
the nave, each labelled with the title of its incumbent. The church's central
entrance porch is housed beneath the tower and is dominated by a statue
of Robert Gray (1787–1838), a testament to the great esteem in which this
former rector was held by his parishioners. The statue was sculpted by David
Dunbar (*c*.1793–1866) of Carlisle in 1838, and stands upon a monumental
plinth. A long, glowing eulogy is inscribed on the base. Gray's outstanding
virtues are celebrated in reliefs of Faith and Charity that stand alongside his
memorial: both are images of women nurturing young children. Mediating
between nave and vestry is a broad narthex, where a robust font stands on
a single baluster of marble. The fluted bowl is surmounted by a vigorous
confection of urns, cherubs' heads and scrolled forms drawn together to form
a canopy. This is part of an elaborate contraption allowing the heavy cover
to be hoisted away from the bowl when baptisms are in progress. The cable
for this mechanism is fed into a tiny dome set into the ceiling. The dome's
inner surface is painted with winged cherubs cavorting in the sky, and its
circumference is ringed with the scripture, 'Suffer the little children to
come unto me and forbid them not for such is the kingdom of God.' [Fig 2]

Holy Trinity was intended to provide church places for the east end of
the town, but by 1764 a new church was proposed as a chapel of ease to Holy
Trinity. *St John the Evangelist in Prospect Row followed the design precepts

2 A miniature painted dome above the font.

of Holy Trinity, though in a more economical form, with much less stonework to relieve the brick. The nave had three tiers, expressed by rows of windows, and a narrow chancel emerged at the east end. Like Holy Trinity, there was a square tower at the west end. The interior had galleries with round-headed arches and paired Ionic columns. The prime mover was John Thornhill (*c.*1720–1802), who owned Thornhill Wharf and whose house in the suburbs gave its name to the present Thornhill area of town. He led the campaign for the new church and attracted many subscribers, as well as giving £4500 of his own money to the project. The dedication to St John and the fact that Thornhill shared the presentation of the living with the bishop shows that he contributed much. He may even have designed the building, as amateur enthusiasts often produced their own designs in the eighteenth century before architecture became a fully professional activity.[8] The foundation stone was laid in 1764 after a grand Masonic procession. The church accommodated 1,200 parishioners; a gallery was provided for Thornhill himself and another for soldiers based at the barracks nearby. Private pews were marked by brass plaques. Despite this, only about half of Thornhill's outlay was recouped in pew rents.[9] When Thornhill died in 1802 he was buried under the altar. St John's was demolished in 1972, but the original organ case is now preserved in Sunderland Museum.

The building of these churches demonstrates that the population of the town was growing rapidly, and there must have been much house building to accommodate the expanding population. Little is known of this as few

3 The interior of Holy Trinity Church.

examples survive. However, we do know that a *Rectory was built in Church Street next to Holy Trinity to designs by William Etty. A number of salubrious merchant houses were also built in Church Street soon after it was laid out in the early eighteenth century. Most were five bays wide and had three storeys, plus a basement. The central bay housed the entrance, which would have had a classical doorcase in either stone or timber. Many of these new houses were built as terraces, but were substantial in their own right. Two large houses of solid design survive to give some idea of what was being built.[10] No. 10 Church Street was built for the merchant John Freeman in 1711 [Fig 4]. The bricks are laid in Flemish bond and the façade is embellished with architectural details in dressed stone (ashlar). The storeys are divided by horizontal string courses. Steps lead up to a recessed central door with an open triangular pediment above and pilasters on either side. Renewed brickwork above the entrance reveals that the house originally had a doorcase with a larger pediment. The house has sash windows typical of the period, and the glazing bars are particularly fine. Above the windows are brick arches with keystones. The two steeply pitched roof ridges are lined with dark slate, but would have been covered with clay pantiles originally.[11] The interior has changed over the years, but retains many significant features. Inside the central passage, most of the doors have architraves and the stairs are framed by an arch with pilasters and keystones. The stairs have stick balusters and a mahogany handrail dating from the early nineteenth century. The use of red brick, sash windows and classical details suggests that these designs were influenced by fashionable developments in London.

This form of early eighteenth-century architecture would later be revived in the Victorian period and came to be known as the Queen Anne style. The buildings surviving in Church Street are typical of the examples that inspired this later resurgence. As the East End of Sunderland declined in importance, however, these houses came to be used as warehouses and workshops. No. 10 was converted into a pub, and is now known as the Hearts of Oak.

Lambton House on nearby High Street was another three-storey, five-bay mansion and was built in about 1737.[12] It was notable for an ornate doorcase in the newly fashionable Baroque style, with a segmental pediment supported by scrolled consoles. The Baroque style was an

4 No. 10 Church Street was built for the merchant John Freeman in 1711. The building is now the Hearts of Oak pub.

exaggerated form of classicism that flourished in seventeenth-century Europe. It was later adopted by English architects such as Wren and Hawksmoor. Lambton House demonstrates that its influence was felt even in the provinces. There were also some mansions built on the outskirts of the town, but these have been demolished: *Herrington Hall, Thornhill (which may have been designed by John Thornhill), *Pallion Hall, *Ford Hall, *High Barnes, *Low Barnes, *Hendon House, *Holme Land, *Bainbridge Holme and *Redby House. These were mainly plain but substantial houses in the currently fashionable style, but their architects or builders are not recorded.[13] High Barnes was built of red brick and had a crude triangular pediment over the entrance. Low Barnes was remodelled in Neoclassical style, with an Ionic portico and giant pilasters.

Among the most impressive of these houses was Ford Hall, built in 1785 [Fig 5]. This was a two-storey, five-bay house with a segmental pediment over the central bay. The entrance boasted a fine semicircular portico on Ionic columns. The house had been owned by John Goodchild, but passed to the Havelock family of shipbuilders. Sir Henry Havelock was born here in 1795, and later won fame as a general in the British Army, helping to quell the Indian Mutiny of 1857. He was commemorated with a statue in Mowbray Park. Ford Hall became the home of William Bell, owner of Monkwearmouth Colliery, but after being sold to Sunderland Council it fell victim to suburban sprawl and was demolished in 1924 to make way for a council housing estate. The newly prosperous coal-fitters built within Sunderland parish

5 One of Sunderland's most impressive early houses, Ford Hall was built in 1785. (Image courtesy of Sunderland Antiquarian Society)

in *Fitters Row, but moved into Bishopwearmouth later in the century and laid out Villiers Street, where some of the terraces remain, some with attractive wooden doorcases. These were probably built by builders acting as their own designers, who would have followed the traditional practices of their trade and used published pattern books for stylistic guidance. Of the houses for the poorer classes few traces survive. No designer would have been involved with the process of subdivision, extension and infilling that produced accommodation for the workers, without whom the prosperity of the merchants and ship owners would not have been possible.

A workhouse was built on the edge of the Town Moor in 1740. This was a plain brick building with steps leading up to a central door between two broad gables. In Sir Francis Eden's report into the state of the poor in 1797 the workhouse was described as being 'in a very good situation. Each apartment has four or five beds with wooden bottoms, and are filled with chaff. Each bed has two blankets, one sheet and rug.'[14] An important survival of Sunderland's early growth is the Donnison School, built alongside the workhouse in Church Walk. This was erected as a girls' school endowed under the will of Elizabeth Donnison in 1764. Thirty-six poor girls were taught reading, writing and arithmetic, as well as needlework. The school is a single-storey building in simple red brick. Like the neighbouring Holy Trinity Church, the bricks were made of clay excavated from the Town Moor. The school was extended in 1827 with a three bay section with round-headed windows and doors.

The commercial buildings that were required to maintain the trade of the port have largely gone. One notable remnant is the Patent Ropery built by Grimshaw and Webster in 1797 at Deptford [Fig 6]. This is the world's oldest

6 Grimshaw and Webster's Patent Ropery at Deptford is the world's oldest factory for machine-made rope.

7 Fulwell Mill was built in about 1821 and is the most complete early windmill in the North East.

factory for machine-made rope, a commodity that was in constant demand in ports such as Sunderland. In 1793 a Sunderland schoolmaster named Richard Fothergill patented a hemp-spinning machine. When Fothergill died, his executor John Grimshaw formed a partnership with Roland Webster, Ralph Hills and Michael Scarth to capitalise on the rights to Fothergill's invention. Webster (1751–1809) was a magistrate and former mayor of Stockton. He provided the finance for the erection of a ropery and gave the building his name. Built on a sloping site, the main block was four storeys tall. It made no concessions to architectural style, but contrived to be entirely satisfying in its proportions. The ropery survives as one of a tiny number of eighteenth-century industrial buildings in Sunderland. The original structure is still recognisable, but numerous alterations and additions have been made, such as the removal of a pediment that once dominated the façade. However, the building retains good cast-iron window frames. The most important feature was of course the newly developed steam-powered machinery that could make rope more efficiently and in greater quantities than traditional methods.[15]

A notable feature of Sunderland's landscape in this period was the proliferation of windmills. There were around a dozen in the district by the early eighteenth century. Many of these were built to a post mill design, which allowed the wooden superstructure to rotate around a large central post. A disadvantage of this design was that high winds could blow the entire structure over, as happened to the old mill at Hendon. A new type of mill was introduced in the seventeenth century, consisting of a substantial stone tower with a revolving cap.[16] Fulwell Mill is an example of this later type [Fig 7]. It was built in about 1821 on the site of an earlier mill in the local magnesian limestone that is so characteristic of Sunderland's vernacular architecture. The tower is built upon a two-storey reefing podium, a high round structure with round-headed doorways at the north and west. These are now blocked, but there are arches at the south and east with metal doors. The base is dressed with brick and the tower is rendered. The tower tapers as it ascends and terminates with a domed cap with sails and a fantail. Fulwell Mill is an important remnant of Sunderland's industrial archaeology, the most complete early windmill in the North East. The structure was restored in 1951 and 1987 and now operates as a museum.

Wearmouth Bridge

The most famous structure in Sunderland was *Wearmouth Bridge, which opened in 1796 [Fig 8]. This was only the second cast-iron bridge in the world and had a span even more daring than that of its predecessor, at Coalbrookdale, Shropshire (1779). To solve the problem of bridging the Wear without interrupting the river traffic and without prohibitive cost, Rowland Burdon (c.1757–1838) was forced to examine the viability of using the untried technology of cast iron. A survey was conducted in 1791, probably by the Bishopwearmouth coal-fitter Thomas Richardson, and the resultant report advised the use of iron. There is much debate about who was responsible for

8 Wearmouth Bridge was designed by Thomas Wilson and opened in 1796. (Image courtesy of Sunderland Public Libraries)

the design of the bridge. The renowned architects Sir John Soane, John Nash and Robert Mylne all offered advice to Burdon. A model made for Thomas Paine of a bridge in America may have been an influence upon Burdon and his supporters. The engineer in charge of the construction process was Thomas Wilson (*c*.1750–*c*.1820), who was born in Monkwearmouth and ran a small mathematical school before taking on the task. Wilson was regarded as a good mathematician and he was also a Freemason, as were many supporters of the project. Wilson was involved with the technical elements of the new bridge from the early stages and came to be the supervisor of the work, living in a house built at the south end of the bridge. He probably did the detailed design with the practical help of the iron founders Walker Brothers of Rotherham and their foreman William Yates, though his name has largely been forgotten. Wilson went on to be involved with the erection of other bridges using the same principles of construction and was regarded as the leading designer of iron bridges, influencing Telford and Rennie. However, Wilson's reputation has not endured because some of his projects ran into technical difficulties, and his bridges at Staines and Yarm both fell.

A river crossing that was not affected by tides and bad weather had immediate benefits for the town. Wearmouth Bridge was a superbly elegant structure, vaulting the river in a single span of 236 ft. The structure consisted of six ribs, each made of 105 cast-iron blocks fixed together by iron rods bolted to grooves in their sides. The bridge was a remarkable feat of engineering, more than double the span of Abraham Darby's bridge in Coalbrookdale, but at 922 tons only three-quarters its weight. The foundation stone was laid amid grand Masonic ceremony in September 1793, indicating how vital Freemasonry had been to the project. A procession of 200 brethren from Phoenix Lodge was led by the provincial grand master, William Henry Lambton. The bridge became a major source of pride to the townsfolk, and its image was reproduced on locally made glassware and pottery. For many years the bridge was a site that warranted travellers making a detour to see it. Subsequently, though, it needed extensive strengthening when unequal expansion of the iron ribs caused buckling. The local engineer John Grimshaw (*c*.1762–1840) reinforced the structure in 1805.[17] In 1853 the abutments of the bridge were damaged by blasting to extend the bottle works on the south-west side. Temporary repairs were made, but further inspection indicated the need to rebuild the bridge. This task was undertaken by the great engineer Robert Stephenson (1803–59) in 1856. His reputation was then at its height after the opening of the Britannia Bridge over the Menai Straits (1846–50). He was in semi-retirement and it was the last project he undertook in Britain. While the design retained several features of the old one it was widened and levelled and lost some of its elegance. It was completed by 1859, though Stephenson was too ill to supervise the work personally. The new bridge proved to be strong enough to bear the tramway system that was introduced in the 1870s and electrified in the early 1900s.[18]

Phoenix Lodge

Freemasonry was integral to the early development of Sunderland, powering many of the enterprises that shaped the town. Freemasonry is a fraternity in which the stonemason's craft and its exalted form – architecture – are used as metaphors for the structure of the universe and form the basis of a moral code. For example, Freemasons must profess a belief in a Supreme Being, who is conceived as the Great Architect of the Universe. Accordingly, Masonic tradition is pervaded by architectural symbolism. Sunderland possesses the oldest Masonic hall still used for its original purpose in the world. Queen Street Masonic Hall is a remarkable survival of Sunderland's early development [Fig 9]. It was built in 1785 to rehouse the King George Lodge, established in 1755. The original building of 1778 was in Vine Street, but this was destroyed by fire on 20 November 1783, which led to a new hall being built. The name Phoenix Lodge was adopted in reference to this resurgence from the flames. The intention was to build a hall similar to the original, and this task was completed by John Bonner (1741–1811), a builder and joiner who was a member of Phoenix Lodge. Bonner was from the family of timber merchants who gave their name to Bonnersfield on the north bank of the Wear, and he is not credited with any other buildings. Therefore he may have used plans from the former building and just supervised the construction, but the external details of the buildings do differ. The hall was built of brick over stone pillars, and these allow for a cellar with an earth floor. The façade is a simple classical design consisting of one tall storey and three bays. Befitting a

9 Queen Street Masonic Hall was designed by John Bonner in 1785.

'society with secrets', the exterior is purposefully inscrutable, faced with plain brick and articulated only with a shallow blind arch and mock windows.[19] The central bay features an aedicule with Masonic symbols – a square and compasses. In Masonic lore the square symbolises morality, and Masons are expected to 'square their actions by the square of virtue'. The compasses signify wisdom of conduct, since Masons are obliged to 'circumscribe their desires and keep their passions within due bounds toward all mankind'.

Despite its unprepossessing exterior, the immaculately preserved interior survives as a monument to Freemasonry and the central role it has played in the development of Sunderland [Fig 10]. It follows the design of the original hall very closely and the splendid fittings were all contemporary. The hall was

10 The interior of Queen Street Masonic Hall, with Master's Throne and sunburst pediment.

11 Mosaic pavement in Queen Street Masonic Hall.

built as a double cube, a form with deep symbolic resonance within Masonic tradition. In this case, the shape was partly dictated by the site, which was previously occupied by a bowling green. The walls are lined with plaster panelling and adorned with gilded symbols and crests, some of which were reproduced from the previous hall. The chairs were acquired from St John's Lodge in Newcastle, which had closed. A dais stands at one end, supporting the master's throne, which is executed in wood with bright gilding. Consisting of a broken pediment on fluted Doric columns, the throne is classical in style and takes a very architectural form, in celebration of the Mason's craft. Masonic symbols are displayed on the frieze. Three alcoves in the rear wall are encapsulated by a round arch on tall Doric columns. These are made from wood but painted to resemble marble, with bright veins of colour running across their surface. The arch is filled with a golden fan-shaped pediment suggesting a sunburst.

At the opposite end of the chamber is an organ gallery bearing a crescent moon emblem in blue and gold. The organ was made by the North East organ builder John Donaldson (d.1807), and is the only example of his work still in its original location. Beneath the organ is another classical throne for the senior warden. Masonic tradition holds that the Temple of Solomon in Jerusalem was decorated with a mosaic pavement of black and white stones. In accordance with this belief, the floor of the hall has a mosaic design with square and compass emblems at the corners [Fig 11]. On the ceiling is a circular emblem with wavering rays of light, at the centre of which is the letter G within an equilateral triangle surrounded by stars. This reputedly represents God as the centre of the universe. The hall has a number of tracing boards – painted panels depicting the various symbols of Freemasonry. These are used as teaching aids when a master explains the concepts of Freemasonry to new members. The tracing boards are in the form of double squares and are infused with mysterious symbolism. One features sun and moon emblems, together with the architectural Orders, stonemasons' implements and a mosaic pavement. Another presents the image of a temple with a golden staircase leading to a corridor, at the end of which is a curtain parted to reveal the letter G. These three panels are pervaded by cryptic letters and numbers.

Sunderland Exchange

A final building that was built at the beginning of the nineteenth century, but which is very much in the eighteenth-century tradition, is the Exchange Building in High Street [Fig 12]. This was one of Sunderland's most important public buildings, serving as public hall, post office, courtroom and market. Built in 1812–14, the Exchange is a plain symmetrical building in a modest classical style. The wide expanse of the façade is modulated by pavilions that project at either end in the Palladian manner. These are surmounted by triangular pediments. A balustrade runs along the roofline and an octagonal clock turret rises at the centre. Nine uniform sash windows run through the first floor above round arches, which were open to allow access to business premises within, linked by Doric pilasters. Clad in stucco, the building presents a gleaming white façade to High Street. The rear and side elevations are of the local magnesian limestone that is so difficult to build with because of its coarse texture. The elegant frontage is indicative of a public building, while the stark elevation at the rear indicates the building's commercial functions.

The Exchange was designed by John Stokoe (*c.*1756–1836) and his son William (*c.*1786–1855), from Newcastle. John Stokoe was the son of a builder who gained his expertise from the building trade rather than formal architectural training. He was probably more of a builder who did some designing, as his father had been, but since a general contractor was also employed (George Cameron of Esk) it is possible that William Stokoe had received some architectural training and

12 Exchange Building by John and William Stokoe, 1812–14.

was trying to establish himself as an architect. Their most important building was the Moot Hall in Newcastle (1810–11), which stands with its huge Greek Doric portico on the banks of the Tyne. Their selection for the Exchange project shows that at this time there was no architect in Sunderland capable of undertaking such an important commission.[20]

When the Exchange was built it assumed many of the secular functions of Holy Trinity Church. By the early nineteenth century the parochial system of local government had become antiquated and untenable. An 1809 Act of Parliament prompted reorganisation, and the local worthies who made up Sunderland's Improvement Commission suggested building the Exchange to serve as Town Hall, post office, Magistrates' Court and market. Funds of nearly £8,000 were raised by public subscription in £50 shares, and a site on High Street East was purchased from Sir Henry Vane Tempest.[21] Once again, the laying of the foundation stone was conducted amid Masonic ceremonies. The Improvement Commissioners occupied the principal rooms on the first floor, which could also be used for public functions. A newsroom offering local and metropolitan papers was included, along with space for magistrates. Behind the arcade was a piazza-like space for markets. The basement contained a watch-house, kitchens and vaults. The Exchange Building was therefore fully equipped for the central role it would play in the administrative and commercial life of the town. Accordingly it was the site of hustings and voting at parliamentary elections.

2

Public Buildings and Services

Victorian Sunderland saw a substantial increase in the provision of services by various forms of public body, and most of these required buildings of some sort. Poor Law Guardians, the Municipal Authority and the School Board were created by Parliamentary powers, but there were also many charities that provided medical care, almshouses and schools. Commercial organisations provided utilities like water and gas, as well as transport improvements such as developments on the River Wear and railways. Many of their requirements were for new types of buildings, and architects had to innovate to meet these new demands. All of these developments had a significant impact on the way in which the fabric of Sunderland was transformed before 1914.

Public Institutions

The most important of these buildings were used by central government. The obscure John Hartforth (1799–*c*.1837), who began as a builder but was described as an architect in a directory of 1834, designed a ★Customs House in 1837. This was modified and supervised in construction by Thompson and Fletcher after Hartforth's early death.[22] The new requirement to register births, marriages and deaths led to Thomas Moore (1796–1869) building a Gothic Register Office on High Street in about 1850; it looks more like a chapel than an office[23] [Fig 13]. This charming oddity was also occupied by the Poor Law Guardians. Moore's true talents lay with classical architecture, as evidenced by his superb design for Monkwearmouth railway station (1848). However, the Register Buildings were designed in a 'Gothick' style typical of the early Gothic Revival, before the grammar of medieval architecture was fully understood. Although the design is somewhat naïve, Gothic was appropriate for a charitable institution such as the Poor Law Guardians, as it evoked the charitable almshouses of the Middle Ages. The building has a symmetrical pointed gable, articulated with three lancet windows. The central lancet is enriched with an intricate finial and quatrefoils. Delicately carved

13 Register Office by Thomas Moore, *c*.1850.

pilasters rise to form octagonal pinnacles, which end with Tudor flowers. This gabled section is flanked by wings that do not have overt Gothic styling and are modest in execution. Nevertheless, it is pleasing that this Gothic relic has survived above the modern shop fronts of High Street West.

The official government architects, the Office of Works, also built in the town. James Williams (1824–92) provided a very old-fashioned looking County Court in John Street in 1875 [Fig 14]. Williams had recently designed Newcastle's General Post Office (1871–4), which demonstrated his highly inventive use of classical forms. In his design for the County Court, however, Williams used a severe Italian Renaissance style. The façade is stern and solemn, with a ground floor of rusticated stone to convey strength. The first floor is of red brick, but with stonework to enliven the windows. Identical doors are placed in the outer bays, and with their massive stone doorcases they echo the neighbouring houses of John Street on a grander scale. Scrolled brackets support entablatures with prominent cornices. Above the door are female heads wearing blindfolds, allegorical representations of justice. The building is crowned with a dentilled entablature and the words 'County Court' are cut into the frieze in stark sans serif letters.

Henry Tanner (1849–1935), who later became chief architect to the Office of Works and received a knighthood, designed a dull but efficient General Post Office and Tax Office on a large site in Sunniside in 1903[24] [Fig 15].

14 County Court by James Williams, 1875.

15 General Post Office and Tax Office by Henry Tanner, 1903.

This was built of golden sandstone with red granite architraves to add colour. The building was designed in an ornate Jacobean style and is very domestic in tone. A profusion of oriel windows makes the first floor rather top heavy, and the façades abound with all manner of projections and recessions. The south face overlooks a public garden. Here, fully rounded Corinthian columns frame the windows of the outer bays. The crowning cornice features an aedicule enclosing the royal coat of arms and a domed lantern rises from the roof ridge. Along West Sunniside, the sorting office is broken into three gables with Diocletian windows, but unfortunately the treatment is rather fragmented.

The Poor Law Guardians were established by the Act of 1834 and initially operated in the existing workhouse in Bishopwearmouth, which they extended and altered until it became clearly inadequate for its function. Acquiring a 7 acre site between Chester Road and Hylton Road, they held a competition in 1853, which was won by Pennington and Jervis of Manchester. The commission was then given to J.E. Oates (1820–69) of York, who had won the second premium. He built a ★Workhouse for 500 paupers to what was the standard design of the time – domestic Tudor with clear separation of the different classes of inmate.[25] For the rest of the century the Guardians made constant additions to the site, and several local architects found work there, including Tillman, Potts, Greener, W.J. Shotton and, most often, the Milburns. None of the additions was anything more than plain and functional, except the Infirmary of 1901–02. The competition in 1893 for the Infirmary was won by Joseph Shields, but he died before building work had started, and W. and T.R. Milburn were invited to construct it. It is not clear whether the attractive brick design with Dutch gables is by Shields or if the Milburns altered the plans.[26] Because of the extensive site, it was possible to develop the workhouse into the current District Hospital after 1930.

The architectural firm established by the Milburn brothers was the most professional in Sunderland. All the family partners received a full architectural training and maintained a varied practice. Significantly, a substantial body of work was undertaken in other parts of the country. William Milburn was born in Sunderland in 1858, the eldest son of William Milburn and Catherine Ridley. His father was a master mariner and a ship owner, who lived at No. 5 The Grove, Ashbrooke. Milburn was educated at the School of Art in Fawcett Street and was articled to John Tillman from 1872 to 1877, before setting up on his own in 1879. In this period he taught in local schools of art, giving classes in Grecian architecture to the Sunderland Students Architectural Association.[27] He was elected a fellow of the Royal Institute of British Architects in 1904 and served on the RIBA Council in 1912–13 as president of the Northern Architectural Association in that year. In 1897 he went into partnership with his brother, Thomas. The firm held several public appointments: Valuer to the Board of Guardians; Valuer to the Rating and Assessment Committee of Sunderland Corporation and Architects to Sunderland Co-operative Society. Milburn was brought up in a Wesleyan household and he was active in the Sans Street Mission, Herrington Street Chapel and St John's Church, Ashbrooke.

Thomas Ridley Milburn was born on 18 October 1862. He also trained with the Tillmans from 1877 to 1882, before becoming an assistant with the practice. He then went to Liverpool and worked for the Corporation on their earliest scheme for building flats, but soon returned to Sunderland to practise on his own in 1887. Among his pupils was Joseph Spain (1871–1935). He joined his brother in partnership in 1897 and continued as a principal of the firm until his death. Exactly which buildings were his responsibility is not clear, but obituaries suggest that he may have done most of the theatre work of the partnership, including the Sunderland Empire (1907). Apart from his design work he was active as an assessor for architectural competitions and was in demand as an arbitrator. He was a committee member of the Northern Architectural Association and served on the RIBA Council for several years, becoming vice-president in 1925–26. He took a special interest in the education of young architects and encouraged the formation of local branches of the NAA on Teesside and in Cumberland. Although brought up as a Wesleyan like his brother, he worshipped at St Michael's Church, Bishopwearmouth, where he served as surveyor to the fabric from 1911 to 1924. He reported on the church around the First World War, and found the first signs of the subsidence that led to the rebuilding by W.D. Caröe (1857–1938).

Up to the First World War the Milburns came close to dominating the profession in Sunderland. The firm gained most of the valuable public commissions before 1914 and went on to become the architects of choice for schools and hospitals. As a result, the firm was one of the largest in the North East in the early twentieth century. The practice was continued by the next generation of the family and survived under the style of W. and T.R. Milburn until it was terminated in 1990.

Charitable Institutions

The provision of hospitals in Sunderland was initially achieved on a voluntary basis with charitable donations, especially from the major employers, who could gain accident treatment for their workers by giving on an annual basis. The first Infirmary was built in 1823 at the bottom of Chester Road by Ignatius Bonomi (1787–1870). This was designed in a domestic style using fashionable brick on the visible façades and coarse limestone on the sides that were hidden from view.[28] In contrast to the Georgian Gothick of Bonomi's later church of St Mary, the Infirmary was designed in his preferred classical style. The present building differs in many details from its appearance when first built. Austere columns and a pediment originally framed the door. Built at a cost of £3,000, the Infirmary had sixty beds, twelve of which were designated for accident victims, twenty for fever victims and twenty-eight for general patients. There was also a rudimentary operating theatre. The Infirmary cared for the sick of Wearside and was particularly important during the cholera epidemic that erupted in 1831. The Infirmary eventually became a Catholic school, and in 1900 the Roman Catholic Education Authority added triangular pediments to the outer pavilions, punctured by *œil de bœuf* windows and surmounted by crosses. These were designed by Charles Walker (1861–1940) of Newcastle, a Roman Catholic architect.

By the 1860s these premises were too small, and Joseph Potts and Son designed a new ★Infirmary on Durham Road [Fig 16]. This was built in 1864–67 with a central administrative and surgical block and two elongated wings, with the wards connected by a long lateral corridor, all in a late medieval domestic style. This commission made the reputation of Potts and Son and set them on their long period of practice.[29] As with the workhouse, later additions by John Eltringham (1854–1933) and especially by the Milburns entirely encased the original building in new extensions so it was no longer visible. The risk of eye injury in the shipyards encouraged the provision of a separate ★Eye Infirmary (1836), again funded by contributions, in High Street. J.W. Donald (1864–1907) of South Shields built a new ★Eye Infirmary on Stockton Road in 1893 in Queen Anne style.[30] Patients with mental health problems had either been sent to the workhouse or to the Durham County Asylum at Sedgfield, but acquiring County Borough status in 1889 meant that Sunderland had to provide its own asylum. In 1891 a competition was held, assessed by C.H. Howell, architect to the Commissioners in Lunacy, for an asylum on 75 acres at Ryhope. The winner was G.T. Hine (1841–1916), a specialist in such designs based in London, and the building, which occupied 5 acres of the site, was erected in 1893–95 at a cost of £63,000.[31] In 1890 an ★Isolation Hospital at the edge of town on Hylton Road was opened to designs by R.S. Rounthwaite (1855–1932), the borough surveyor. This complex of five blocks was built within 12 acre grounds and included three isolated pavilions for patients with infectious diseases.[32] In 1907 Thomas Young (b.1862), surveyor to Sunderland Rural District Council, added an ★Isolation Hospital for RDC residents on the same site. The emphasis was on practicality rather than aesthetic appeal.[33] Finally, a Children's Hospital was built on Durham Road on land donated by the Pemberton family (1908–12). In the competition of 1907 the first premium went to Armstrong and Wright of Newcastle, but by the time tenders were being sought the Milburns were in charge of the project. The reason for the change is unknown. The Milburns provided an attractive design for a central administrative block and wards in pavilions, all with classical detailing.[34]

As well as hospitals, provision was made for the elderly and orphans. As a port, Sunderland had many aged or sick mariners to care for, as well as their wives, widows and children. Sailors had compulsory deductions taken from their pay and these were paid into a seamen's fund known as the Muster Roll to

16 Sunderland Infirmary, Durham Road by Joseph Potts and Son, 1864–67.

provide pensions. In 1840 this fund was used to build Trafalgar Square in Church Walk, a complex of fourteen almshouses for 104 elderly merchant seamen and their widows [Fig 17]. Trafalgar Square was built on the site of the workhouse garden by the trustees of the Muster Roll, which was administered through the Customs House. It was of course named after Nelson's legendary naval victory of 1805, at which seventy-six sailors from Sunderland were present. Surprisingly, however, Sunderland's Trafalgar Square is older than its more famous namesake; it was opened five years before London's Trafalgar Square was completed.

The almshouses were probably designed by William Drysdale (1793–1856), a builder and surveyor who acted for the Corporation on occasion. The two-storey houses are built around three sides of a quadrangle, framing an attractive garden. The fourth side of the square is marked by a wall and railings. The houses are executed in plain brick laid in English garden wall bond, with stone dressings over the white-painted sash windows. The central door is set within a round-headed brick arch, beneath an overlight with radial glazing bars. The narrow corner bays are canted, and the rear elevations are now rendered with pebbledash. The central block boasts commemorative plaques and heraldic emblems [Fig 18]. A large plaque records the building of the almshouses and bears the inscription: 'Trafalgar Square, erected by the Trustees of the Muster Roll Anno Domini 1840, under the 4TH and 5TH of William IV.' Above this is a brightly painted plaque with relief figures of a sailor and lion holding escutcheons and maritime symbols, together with royal coats of arms. Around one of the escutcheons is written 'Tria Juncta in Uno' (three joined in one). This is the motto of the Order of the Bath, of which Nelson was a member. Surmounting the whole composition is the famous signal sent by Nelson at the Battle of Trafalgar, 'England expects every man to do his duty.' A flagpole secured with mooring ropes stands in the grounds, evoking the dangerous occupation of Trafalgar Square's first residents. There is also a lampholder in the centre of the

17 Trafalgar Square almshouses by William Drysdale, 1840.

garden, standing upon an ashlar base and plinth with cast-iron lamp brackets. Surprisingly, Trafalgar Square has survived and is still in residential use.[35]

Later in the period the Mowbray Almshouses were built on an elevated site on Bishopwearmouth Green, forming an impressive group with St Michael's Church. Jane Gibson, the widow of a local merchant, had built a complex of almshouses on this site in 1727; Elizabeth Gray Mowbray funded the building of the present almshouses in 1863. The new buildings were an early design by the Durham-born architect Edward Robert Robson (1836–1917). Robson began his training under the tutelage of John Dobson in Newcastle, before entering the office of Sir George Gilbert Scott (1811–78), one of the most productive architects of the Victorian era. Robson practised as architect to Durham Cathedral for six years, before being appointed architect and surveyor to the Corporation of Liverpool in 1864. However, Robson was best known as the first architect to the London School Board, in which role he developed influential models for the design of urban board schools. He became the pre-eminent school architect of his generation and published a substantial book on the subject.[36]

The Mowbray Almshouses were built during Robson's tenure as architect to Durham Cathedral, when he was in partnership with John Wilson Walton (1823–1910) [Fig 19]. The buildings are strongly Gothic in style, and follow Pugin's notion of recreating a medieval almshouse. The block has an L-shaped plan, as well as a forecourt framed by walls and railings. There are four houses in total, each of two storeys. Each has a central door set

18 Commemorative plaque at Trafalgar Square almshouses.

within a pointed arch. The doors are flanked by gables with pointed arches and two-light windows. The second house is built at the corner, and for this reason the door is set within a canted corner bay. The steeply pitched roof has tall chimneys along the ridge. The almshouses are built from thin courses of squared sandstone rubble, but there are some decorative details in dressed stone. The gables terminate with clove-shaped finials. At the left-hand side is a stepped chimney-stack with a Latin inscription commemorating Jane Gibson's laying of the original foundation stone in 1727 and Elizabeth Gray Mowbray's rebuilding in 1863. The right-hand chimney-stack displays the Mowbray lion in low relief under a dripmould with fleur-de-lys finial.

As well as aiding mariners, Sunderland had to provide for their orphans and illegitimate children. Sunderland's Orphan Asylum was begun in 1856 on the Town Moor and opened in 1860 [Fig 20]. It was funded from the proceeds of selling access rights on the Town Moor to railway companies. The design was the result of an architectural competition in which the firm of Childs and Lucas came second. Nevertheless, their designs were eventually selected. As a London-based practice, however, their role in the construction process was minimal, and construction was instead supervised by the local architect Thomas Moore.

The orphanage was designed in the Italian Renaissance style fashionable in the 1860s. The most prominent feature is the Italianate belvedere tower, which was based on the towers at Osborne House, Queen Victoria's summer

19 Mowbray Almshouses by E.R. Robson, 1863. The Gothic design evokes the charitable almshouses of the Middle Ages.

residence on the Isle of Wight (1845–51). Osborne House had been designed by Prince Albert (something of an architectural aficionado) in conjunction with the builder Thomas Cubitt. The building spawned a number of provincial imitations, particularly its distinctive tower. In a further connection with the monarchy, Victoria herself donated £100 towards construction of the orphanage and asked to see the architectural plans. The orphanage is a two-storey brick building with a central tower built over the entrance. Paired Renaissance arches lead to a porch in the base of the tower, and a roundel window occurs in the spandrel between them. The upper section of the tower has three round-headed arches, affording a fair view or 'belvedere' of the port and the sea. The tower ends with a low pyramidal roof. As was typical of Renaissance-style buildings the storeys increase in grandeur as they ascend. The windows in the ground floor are set within plain round-headed arches, but the first floor has more elaborate windows with segmental architraves and keystones. A cornice supported on brackets runs around the whole building. Although the orphanage was designed in a fashionable Italianate style, the overall effect is severe and institutional. Opening on 17 October 1861, the orphanage was able to accommodate forty boys at a time. It was intended to train them for a career at sea, and for this reason the inmates' uniform was a sailor suit.[37]

Other substantial buildings commissioned by charitable organisations were the ★Sunderland Sailors' Home of 1856 by James Gillis Brown (1830–1890)[38]

20 Sunderland Orphan Asylum by Childs and Lucas, 1856–60.

and the ornamental Gothic ★Pottery Buildings (1868) in High Street East, which were paid for by the Backhouse family to act as a community centre for the East End [Fig 21]. This was the first local design by Frank Caws (1846–1905), when he was working as managing clerk for Potts and Son.[39] The buildings were named after a pottery that had occupied the same site. Another example was the Blind Institute in Villiers Street of 1882, which was built by J. and T. Tillman in brick and, unusually for the period, in a classical style.[40]

The Tillmans had a prolific practice in Sunderland. John Tillman (1835–99) was the son of John Tillman Sr, who died in Sulina, Romania, in 1869. All the family hailed from Sunderland, and after 'practical training' John was articled to Martin Greener from 1854 to 1857. He remained with Greener as managing clerk until August 1859 and was principally engaged on houses and chapels, but he did spend some time travelling in Britain and Europe. He entered independent practice in October 1859 at No. 5 Bridge Street, and was joined by his brother Thomas on 1 January 1875. He was a Freemason in the No. 949 Williamson Lodge and was involved in the formation of Fenwick Lodge in 1872. He died in lodgings at Harrogate on 31 December 1899 and was buried in the family grave in Sunderland Cemetery. He never married. Thomas Tillman was born on 31 March 1852 and trained in his brother's firm from 1866 to 1871. He remained there as chief assistant until 1874 and became a partner on 1 January 1875, staying until his death on 24 June 1892 in London from the effects of rheumatic fever. He was also unmarried and, as his sister and her only child predeceased him, there was no generation to succeed the brothers.

The Tillmans were the first firm in Sunderland to operate in a fully professional manner, with both brothers being elected to the RIBA. They were also important as trainers of younger architects, including the Milburns, G.T. Brown, John Hall and Harry Barnes. Despite this, the practice remained almost wholly local and relatively small scale. Their major project was the Museum of 1879, for which they used a French-inspired classical design. The rest of the practice was heavily reliant on the design of chapels for various Nonconformist groups; they produced at least twenty-four in a simple and cheap style. Some were effective, like the Hood Street Chapel built by the United Methodist Free Church, but they were largely anonymous. Tatham Street Primitive Methodist Chapel was a grander design in a Lombardic style, which led several church members to withdraw in protest against the extravagance of the project and to form the Christian Lay Church. In later years the Tillmans undertook some more prestigious commissions, such as the High Schools, the Blind Institute and business premises in the town centre. They also acted as surveyors to Sunderland Rural Sanitary Authority.

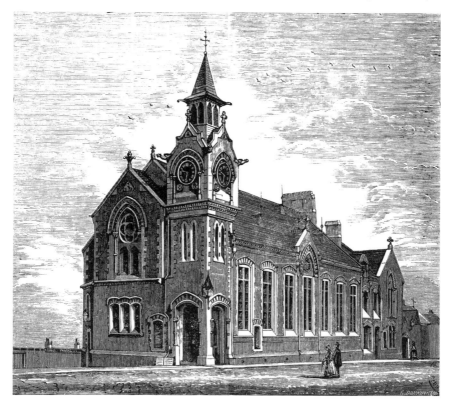

21 The former Pottery Buildings, High Street East, by Frank Caws, 1868. (Image courtesy of Sunderland Museum)

Local Government Enterprises

In spite of all the laudable activity of other bodies, the main provider of services in the town was the Municipal Authority, created in 1836 and given full powers in 1851, when it took over the functions of the Improvement Commissioners. The main driver of action was the need to improve public health conditions in Sunderland, which were as bad as in most industrial towns. The implementation of the Public Health Act in 1851 demanded the appointment of a borough surveyor to plan a drainage and sewerage scheme and to administer the process of approving plans for new buildings in accordance with the building regulations. The man appointed was a native of Sunderland, William Crozier (1829–1905). Aged twenty-two, he had only just completed his articles with Robert Nicholson CE in Newcastle. He surveyed and mapped Sunderland, making the first proper trigonometric survey of the town at a scale of 44ft to the inch, and then planned a drainage scheme for the Borough. Feeling that he had proved his worth, he asked for an increase in salary. When this was denied he moved to become county surveyor of Durham, in which post he remained until his retirement in 1888. In Durham, Crozier had wider responsibilities than in Sunderland, involving highways and bridges as well as designing buildings for official use. He also maintained a large private practice until 1886. Elected to the Northern Architectural Association in 1865, his standing in the profession was marked when he was granted life membership of the Institution of Civil Engineers. His work on the Assize Courts in Newcastle and Durham was praised by the great Victorian architects Alfred Waterhouse, George Gilbert Scott and George Edmund Street, the last of whom used them as guides when designing the Royal Courts of Justice in London (1868–82). For the sake of a small sum, Sunderland had lost one of the most distinguished local government surveyors of his generation.[41]

Crozier's deputy Thomas Younger (1809–79) was promoted to the vacant position at the old salary, but his background of managing building firms meant that he was unable to undertake much design work.[42] While the surveyor was responsible for the sewage system, the water that was needed to make it work was provided by the private Sunderland and South Shields Water Company. They used Thomas Hawksley (1807–1903) of Nottingham and London as their consulting engineer, and he advised them to pump water from underground aquifers into holding reservoirs and then to use gravity to distribute the water to homes. Beginning practice in his native Nottingham in 1830, Hawksley was the best-known water engineer in the country, responsible for over 150 schemes in Britain and abroad. In Sunderland, as well as the hidden pipe works he designed twelve pumping stations from Humbledon in 1846 to Stoneygate in 1905. All are substantial brick buildings and they are all slightly different in style. Humbledon was a utilitarian two-storey building with a single-storey block at the rear surmounted by a chimney. Ryhope (1866–69) is the best

known, as its steam engines are preserved and open to the public[43] [Fig 22].
The building consists of an engine house and boiler house with a prominent
chimney. Executed in brick with stone dressings, the principal buildings have
a grand entrance stair and shaped gables arrayed with finials. The interior
is a remarkably well-preserved monument to the Age of Steam, with its
machinery in gleaming brass and steel. The various buildings are set within
landscaped grounds with a rectangular pond. The engines were built by R. and
W. Hawthorn of Newcastle.

The one Water Company building Hawksley did not design was the Head
Office in John Street, which opened in 1907 to designs by W. and T.R. Milburn
[Fig 23]. This was designed in the Baroque style favoured during the Edwardian
period, but executed in red sandstone from Penrith, which gives the building
a lush colour unusual for its date.[44] Porches project from the outer bays, each
ornamented with Ionic columns and a segmental pediment. The ground
floor has round-headed windows in hollow reveals with elaborately scrolled
keystones. At first-floor level the windows are framed with delicate aedicules.
The main elevation to Borough Road is divided by unusual chamfered pilasters
that end with richly carved drapery and cartouches. Unlike many other towns,
Sunderland Corporation did not municipalise the Water Company, but they
did take over the Sunderland Gas Company. Hawksley was also consulting
engineer for this enterprise, as he was experienced in this field as well, being

22 Ryhope Pumping Station by Thomas Hawksley, 1866–69. This is one of twelve such
buildings across Sunderland designed by Hawksley.

the first president of the Gas Managers' Association. The Hendon Gas Works was built in 1860, and extended in 1870 by Hawksley.[45]

Two other pressing health issues were provision for burying the dead and organising washing and bathing facilities for those houses not yet connected to the water supply. The Corporation was involved in both these areas, though it was Burial Boards who initially constructed the cemeteries. In 1849 Bishopwearmouth Church opened Rector's Gill Cemetery in order to relieve the churchyard. This was funded by the bishopric and designed by Thomas Moore.[46] All three parishes in Sunderland had cemeteries laid out in the 1850s, but these were located at inconvenient distances from the main housing districts. In each case private architects designed the layout, entrance lodges and two mortuary chapels for Anglican and Nonconformist use in what was the conventional style of the period. In 1856 Thomas Moore designed Bishopwearmouth Cemetery on Chester Road at the high cost of £17,000; this was because of the difficulty in finding a large enough site.[47] Sunderland Parish found a site on Ryhope Road, and in 1858 Matthew Thompson (c.1822–78) of Newcastle brought in his design for less than the estimate at £7000.[48] Mere Knolls Cemetery was built at Seaburn, and Thomas Oliver (1824–1902) provided a slightly more ornate group of buildings in 1855–56.[49] The opening of these cemeteries enabled all the churchyards in the town to be closed. Later cemeteries were created for Southwick in 1884 and for Ryhope in 1898.

23 Water Company Offices by W. and T.R. Milburn, 1907.

Thomas Oliver was also heavily involved with the provision of public baths and wash-houses in the town. The first of these was opened in ★Hendon Road in 1851. When Oliver was criticised for the costs of his design he wrote a defence in the local press, in which he claimed that his first three designs of 1848–50 had been rejected by the Baths Committee and that he had therefore received no fee. He also visited baths elsewhere in the country, and so when he finally received his fee he calculated on the basic cost of the building that he was £50 out of pocket, even though he had designed one of the cheapest and most profitable baths in the country, from which the ratepayers were getting extremely good value.[50] His annoyance was enhanced when William Crozier used the basic elements of Oliver's design to build ★public baths in 1853–54 on the estate owned by Sir Hedworth Williamson (1797–1861) in Monkwearmouth and also on ★High Street West in 1858–59.[51] Oliver did, however, produce a book on the subject, which helped him to win commissions for at least seven schemes around the country in the next decade.[52] The Corporation continued to upgrade these facilities with the construction of ★swimming baths in High Street (1890), designed by R.S. Rounthwaite, who was surveyor from 1879 to 1898, and the rebuilding of Oliver's original ★Hendon Baths (1903–06) by J.W. Moncur (c. 1860–1920), surveyor from 1900 to 1920, in collaboration with Brown and Spain.[53]

The Corporation remained active in the crucial fields of public health and the maintenance of roads and footpaths. It was able to provide facilities of a less basic nature, especially as the century went on and permissive legislation widened the range of services that could be offered. Among these was the creation of public parks, which were initially seen as an adjunct to better health but later became places of resort for citizens. Through the provision of arboreta and labelled planting they also served as places of instruction about the natural world. Despite the availability of the seaside, development eroded traditional open spaces like Bishopwearmouth Green and the Town Moor. This made the establishment of public open space a necessity. Sunderland's first park was created by adapting the quarry on Building Hill into a series of walks that made use of the irregular terrain to provide visual interest. The Corporation had purchased the land in 1852 from the Mowbray Estate, and sought to extinguish the rights of copyholders to quarry stone without charge. The eastern portion was laid out by Mr Lawson, gardener to Lord Londonderry. The ★West Park across Burdon Road was laid out by Robert Smith, who had worked at Chatsworth as an assistant to Joseph Paxton, England's best-known park designer. Mowbray Park opened in 1857, with a bandstand and lodge house designed by William Crozier.[54] A major debate then ensued about the cost of extending the park northwards across the railway line and up to Borough Road. This was only resolved by a public inquiry. In 1864 a competition was held, the winners being Thomas Angelo Moore (1840–91), the architect son of Thomas Moore Sr, and Robert Humphrey CE.

However, Councillor James Lindsay (1821–1900), a carver and gilder, was an active campaigner for the park and had been excluded from the competition because of his membership of the council. He submitted a plan for the park which contained many of the ideas in Moore and Humphrey's design, though he claimed that it had been drawn before the competition was judged. Moore and Humphrey printed a handbill disputing this claim, but the park was laid out to Lindsay's plans, which included the terrace and screening of trees to conceal the railway line, a bridge to connect the extension to the original park and an ornamental lake with an island for nesting wildfowl. A strip of land fronting Borough Road was left as grass to allow the Corporation to build on it in the near future, and Councillor William Donkin produced a wild design for council offices, public hall, museum and art gallery based on Paxton's Crystal Palace. The opening in July 1866 involved a procession of 17,000 Sunday School children, watched by 20,000 inhabitants, and was the subject of a long and extraordinarily positive report in the *Sunderland Times*.[55] Further parks were laid out. In 1880 Roker Park was created on land donated by Sir Hedworth Williamson. This was also designed by James Lindsay, who was now an alderman and Chair of the Parks Committee, in conjunction with the council's head gardener, Mr Johnson. It included a lake for the growing number of model yacht enthusiasts in the town who had lost their pond on the Town Moor.[56] Unemployment problems led to a competition to improve the seafront at Roker to provide work. T.R. Milburn won with a scheme that created a promenade and some facilities for visitors, including restaurants, shops, covered shelters and bazaars. These were built of cement and iron with zinc roofs.[57] J.W. Moncur, borough surveyor, and Henry Hay Wake (1844–1911), River Wear Commission engineer, extended this in 1907.[58] Barnes Park was laid out in 1907–09 on the grounds of Low Barnes, a Pemberton family house, by J.W. Moncur and W. Hall, the parks superintendent. This too was an unemployment relief scheme.[59]

The space left vacant in Mowbray Park came to be the centre of the council's worst-handled building project, though it did finally become the site of one of the town's most important buildings. The need for a Town Hall and Municipal Offices had been raised regularly, and had been deferred on the grounds of cost and the difficulty of finding a suitable site. In 1872 the need for a large public hall was met by the building of the ★Victoria Hall in Toward Road with the backing of the Backhouse family [Fig 24]. Designed by their usual architect, G.G. Hoskins (1837–1911) of Darlington, this was a large brick building in the Gothic style, with an L-shaped plan and a prominent tower at the corner. The tower ended with battlements, pinnacles and a spire. Venetian Gothic arches and polychrome brick and stone aligned the building with the High Victorian Gothic mode. The west face of the building was left blank to allow for extension at a later date. The interior had two tiers of seating on slender cast-iron columns and the ceiling was braced with beams resting on corbels. However, the Victoria Hall was the site of a disaster in 1883 when 183 children were crushed and suffocated to death in a rush to get prizes at a children's show. The disaster resulted in new legislation demanding outward-opening exits for all such places of entertainment. The Hall was acquired by the Corporation in 1903 and they built an extension, ★Edward Hall, which opened in 1906. This was designed in a matching style by John Eltringham, and featured a polygonal tower and spire.[60] However, the Victoria Hall was destroyed by a parachute mine in 1941, and because of its notorious history it was not lamented.

In 1874 a competition was held for a Town Hall on two possible sites in Mowbray Park. The outcome was an embarrassment to all. Two winners were announced, but as no assessor had been appointed the profession was hugely critical of the process. The favourite design was that by Frank Caws, but this was disqualified on the grounds of exceeding the stated cost [Fig 25]. There was then a legal challenge to the site by members of the council, which found that the park was meant to be open freely to citizens in perpetuity and that council offices would infringe this. The whole scheme was abandoned and the council was humiliated.[61]

Another attempt was made in 1886, when a competition for a site on the Shrubbery in Fawcett Street was announced. Alfred Waterhouse, architect of Manchester Town Hall, was the assessor. This was for ★Municipal Offices and Council Chamber, and the winner was Brightwen Binyon (1846–1905), who practised in Ipswich. Binyon had been a pupil in Waterhouse's office in Manchester and so was known to the assessor. Although none of the entrants

24　Victoria Hall by G.G. Hoskins, 1872. (Image courtesy of Sunderland Antiquarian Society)

really solved the noise problems caused by Fawcett Street at the front and the railway station at the rear, the winning design came to be held in great affection by Sunderland residents. The building was in a French-inspired classical style with a prominent clock tower, though this style was in part demanded by the requirement to be in keeping with the neighbouring buildings in the street.[62] [Fig 26]. The building had two storeys, plus an attic inside the Mansard roof – such features were the hallmark of the French Renaissance style and were named after the French architect François Mansart (1598–1666). The clock tower stood at the centre above the entrance and terminated with a cupola dome and lantern. The entrance was set within a round arch beneath an overhanging balcony and central window. Projecting outer pavilions with columned façades added grandeur. The long street frontage was enriched with medallions, carved panels and floriated capitals to the columns. The building housed a number of lavish interiors, including a grand staircase and council chamber[63] [Fig 27]. Overall, Binyon's design was not very distinguished, but it gave dignity to the street. When it was opened in 1890 and formally named the Town Hall it was almost immediately found to be too small. An extension was sought in 1904, and the competition was won by Wills and Anderson of London with a façade that was identical to the existing building. It was never built.[64]

The building that was finally erected on the Mowbray Park site was the Museum, Art Gallery, Library and Winter Garden, which did not infringe the covenants affecting the park because it was freely open to visitors. Sunderland was the first authority outside London to run a museum under

25 Frank Caws's design for a Town Hall in Mowbray Park, 1874. This design was never executed and a Town Hall was eventually built to different designs on another site. (Image courtesy of Sunderland Museum)

26 Sunderland Town Hall by Brightwen Binyon, 1886–90. (Image courtesy of Sunderland Museum)

the Museums Act of 1845, when it took over the collections of the Sunderland Natural History and Antiquarian Society, which were housed in the Athenaeum in Fawcett Street. The classical *Athenaeum had been built in 1840 to designs by William Billinton (1807–60) of Wakefield [Fig 28]. Intended for the residents of the Fawcett Estate, it provided a reading room and halls for the meetings of local societies. It was an austere rectangular building, only relieved by an Ionic portico, but the monumental pediment was perhaps too heavy for the design. The outer bays projected slightly and were emphasised with stark pilasters. The Athenaeum was demolished and replaced by a Liberal Club (1900) designed by John Eltringham. This was funded by rent from shops on the ground floor.[65]

Edward Backhouse proposed to build a 'Crystal Palace' on Building Hill, which would have included space for the museum. This scheme came to nothing and in 1876 a competition for a new building was won by J. and T. Tillman. Their building, which opened in 1879, strives for monumentality, but the design seems ponderous and pretentious [Fig 29]. The style is eclectic, merging grand classical elements with the French Renaissance style, which had a sporadic influence on British architecture in the 1870s and '80s. The style figured prominently in the North East, with both the Bowes Museum at Barnard Castle (begun 1869) and Newcastle and Gateshead Gas Company Offices (1884–86) invoking the image of French châteaux. Sunderland Museum was probably influenced by the Bowes Museum, which was built by the art collectors John and Josephine Bowes and designed by the French architect Jules Pellechet.[66] Sunderland Museum's classical ambitions are propounded by a powerful central block that takes the

27 The Council Chamber of Sunderland Town Hall. (Image courtesy of Sunderland Museum)

28 The former Athenaeum by William Billinton, 1840. (Image courtesy of Sunderland Antiquarian Society)

form of a Roman triumphal arch. Within this arch is suspended a balcony over two rather insignificant doors. The block climaxes in a French Mansard roof and is flanked by two-storey side wings. The ground floor is expressed by pedimented windows, but the upper storey is encased in heavy ornamentation with a grand Corinthian order for the phalanx of squat columns. The outermost bays are pushed forward and emphasised by vertical strips of banded rustication and finished with diminutive Mansard roofs, which seem too narrow to justify this treatment. US President Ulysses S. Grant was present at the laying of the foundation stone by Alderman Samuel Storey in 1877. Immediately behind the museum were the Winter Gardens. These were built of cast-iron and glass, mirroring the form of the main building. Unfortunately they were destroyed by a parachute mine during an enemy bombing campaign in 1941.[67] The nearby Victoria Hall was destroyed in the same attack.

Sunderland was also in need of libraries. Before the nineteenth century reading had been a socially exclusive practice, with both literacy and access to reading materials being restricted to the upper and middle classes. Improvements in education facilitated the spread of literacy among the working classes, but even after the benefits of the 1870 Elementary Education Act began to be felt the cost of books prevented many working people from reading. To meet the new demand for reading matter, libraries and reading rooms sprang up in major towns and cities. The public library cause was mainly promoted by middle-class philanthropists who were concerned by conditions among Britain's labouring population and believed that the accumulation of wealth gave them a moral obligation to help those less fortunate than themselves.

At the beginning of the twentieth century Sunderland used money awarded by the Scottish-born industrialist Andrew Carnegie (1835–1919) to build three branch libraries. All the commissions were won in competition and had to follow a basic plan produced by the Borough librarian, John Alfred Charlton Deas (1874–1951).[68] As a result, the three libraries are remarkably similar. Edward Cratney (1882–1916) of Wallsend designed two of them – Hendon in 1908 and Monkwearmouth in 1909.[69] Hendon Branch Library was confidently placed on a corner site, the frontage cutting across the junction and the wings running back along divergent streets. The entrance is cut into a heavily rusticated arch set within a thrusting porch. The building terminates with monumental square pediments and the words 'Branch Library' are displayed on a stone panel. The upper portion of the walls was lined with masonry pierced by *œil de bœuf* windows amid ornate swags of drapery. Of the three Carnegie libraries in Sunderland, Hendon was perhaps the most successful in architectural terms.

Monkwearmouth Branch Library was designed by Cratney and was closely akin to his earlier design for Hendon [Fig 30]. The façade is slightly concave and the outer bays have dramatic Diocletian windows below broad open pediments. The central block has a raised door framed by strong stone

29 Sunderland Museum by J. and T. Tillman, 1876–79.

30 Monkwearmouth Branch Library by Edward Cratney, 1908–09.

pilasters, which support a dentilled entablature. A stolid square pediment rises above the entrance, with the words 'Branch Library' cut into its surface. Internally, the roof is supported by fat Doric columns. A brass plaque commemorates Andrew Carnegie's donation. The foundation stone was laid on 20 January 1908 and commemorates Arthur F. Young, Mayor of Sunderland, as well as J.A. Charlton Deas. The stone also declares that the site was the gift of John George Addison JP, former vice-chairman of the Libraries, Museums and Art Gallery Committee. The contractor was Joseph Huntley.

Sunderland architect Hugh Taylor Decimus Hedley (1866–1939) designed the West Branch Library in Kayll Road (1909) [Fig 31]. The site was donated by Alderman William Burns JP and the contractor was W.B. Cooper. Like the others, the library is a diminutive single-storey building in the Baroque style. The central porch has a dentilled ogee pediment resting upon columns with jutting blocks of rustication. This device is known as a Gibbs surround, after the Baroque architect James Gibbs (1682–1754). The words 'Branch Library' are incised below the pediment and the date 1909 is displayed within. The outer wings are emphasised by stone pilasters with block rustication. Rich cartouches bearing the arms of the Borough occur within open pediments. Again, many towns and cities of this period relied on private philanthropy to provide public amenities such as libraries. As these were seen as vital assets to the town, however, municipal authorities were keen to publicise their own role in providing them. By marking the libraries with the Borough arms, Sunderland Corporation defined them as products of its own enterprise. Sculptural embellishment is complemented

31 West Branch Library in Kayll Road by H.T.D. Hedley, 1909.

by rich colouring; the bright red brick contrasts with masses of buff sandstone. The door is panelled and, like many nineteenth-century doors in Sunderland, the central panels are circular. Commemorative stones at left and right list the donor of the site, the architect and town clerk, along with the contractor, mayor and officials. Sunderland's three Carnegie libraries were among the first to offer open access to the shelves for borrowers.

One further large scheme was undertaken by the Corporation, and again they held a national competition. This was to make more effective provision for the police and fire services and to build a new Police Court. Plans from as far back as 1840 had come to nothing, and the police were based in two adapted houses in East Cross Street. The Court was in Bridge Street. The site next to the Volunteer Drill Ground at the west end of High Street was a difficult one, as there were existing properties which were not acquired when the competition was announced in 1902. While the assessor, J.S. Gibson, was complimentary about the entries, the competition did not attract many distinguished architects. The winners were W. and T.R. Milburn with Wills and Anderson of London. It is not clear who did exactly what in the design process, but the Milburns certainly supervised the construction and in the town they were always seen as the architects of the scheme. The assessor emphasised the practical merits of the design and paid particular attention to Home Office guidelines on the design of cells and access routes in the Court building, rather than to the visual appeal of the building.

The Police Station and Magistrates' Court stands on a prominent site on Gill Bridge Avenue [Fig 32]. Designed in full-blown Edwardian Baroque

32 Police Station and Magistrates' Court by W. and T.R. Milburn in collaboration with Wills and Anderson of London, 1902.

33 Fire Station by W. and T.R. Milburn in collaboration with Wills and Anderson, 1902.

34 Flaming torch emblems at the Fire Station.

style, the building has the decorative flair typical of the period, but as a building for the dispensation of justice many of its features are stern and monumental. Responding to the awkward site, the architects produced an asymmetrical composition, with three bays projecting at the left under a triangular pediment and a tower rising at the right. In true Baroque fashion the ground-floor windows are fortified with Gibbs surrounds, and rich cartouches occur between the windows. The entrance is set in the base of the tower and consists of a robust panelled door flanked by Ionic columns. The tower itself is a sophisticated composition, with a tall second stage featuring clock-faces and festoons of flowers. The tower culminates with a lantern of square columns supporting volutes and a ball finial. Beyond the principal façade, the building takes on a stern dignity symbolising the authority of the law. Much of the masonry is plain and severe, although the central block is enriched with *œil de bœuf* windows. In a bold gesture, the rear elevation has Diocletian windows, a motif derived from the gigantic thermae or baths of Ancient Rome. The foundation stone was laid by Councillor J.C. Kirtley JP, chairman of the Watch Committee, on 18 January 1905, and construction was carried out by J.W. White. Despite its shortcomings, the building presents an imposing frontage to people coming up High Street. The Fire Station has a more whimsical appearance, with the decorative flambeaux over the doors. Giant pilasters divide the façade, and the five central bays have interlinked rusticated arches, through which fire engines once rushed out. Executed in brick, it is quite different from the main block, which is in stone[70] [Fig 33 & 34].

Schools

The provision of schools was not the responsibility of the Corporation until the Education Act of 1904, and indeed not of any public body until the Education Act of 1870 established School Boards. Before this the main players in schooling in Sunderland were private schools and the churches. The best-known private school in the town was Dr Cowan's School at the ★Grange, which operated in a converted house from 1830.[71] Sunderland Girls' High School was built in Mowbray Road in 1888 to designs by the Tillmans. A more short-lived Boys' High School operated in Park Place East.[72] The churches took their responsibilities seriously, creating national societies to assist localities in building schools. The Church of England had the target of opening a school in every parish. In Sunderland, the first of these was in Bishopwearmouth in 1808. Southwick National School was designed by John Hartforth (1799–1836) and opened in 1837.[73] Large schools were built in Sunderland Parish and Bishopwearmouth by architects who were much involved with church building. The ★Gray Schools for Holy Trinity Church were designed in 1856–57 by Thomas Austin (1822–67) of Newcastle, whose distinguished career was cut short by illness. The ★Rectory Schools for St Michael's Church were designed in 1854 by John Dobson, and then substantially extended by George Andrew Middlemiss (1815–87) in 1866.[74] Nonconformists, in addition to their many Sunday Schools, built a British and Foreign Society School in Borough Road in 1858–59. This was designed by Joseph Potts and Son, and was often called the Quaker School because the Backhouses had been the prime movers of the scheme.[75] There were also some examples of schools being provided by employers. Thomas Austin built the Colliery Schools at Monkwearmouth in 1861 and William Forster (1832/3–97) designed *schools in Silksworth for Lord Londonderry when his colliery was operational in 1876.[76] But it was the creation of Sunderland School Board in 1870 that gave architects real opportunities to win commissions and to gain expertise in the design of schools.

By the mid-nineteenth century it was widely recognised that elementary education in Britain was inadequate. The massive population increase associated with industrialisation meant that two-thirds of British children received no educational instruction whatsoever, and existing schools could not possibly meet the increasing demand. In 1870 Gladstone's Liberal government passed the Elementary Education Act, which promised a standardised system of education. The Act initiated a nationwide programme of school-building that was to be administered by parochial or municipal School Boards. These were charged with an important social mission, and it was soon recognised that a consistent architectural strategy based upon sound principles was required. The Durham-born architect E.R. Robson was appointed architect and surveyor to the London School Board in 1871, and began to formulate a more rigorous approach.[77] He conducted a study of schools on the Continent and in America, and his findings were published in *School Architecture* (1874), a book that was highly influential. Robson's principles shaped the official policy of the London School Board, which built 289 schools between 1870 and 1884. His influence was increased when he became consultant architect to the Government Education Board and had to approve all designs before they got financial sanction. He was also the assessor in many school competitions. The influence of the London Board Schools was therefore felt throughout the country. The architectural style chosen to express the ideals of the Elementary Education Act was Queen Anne, which was thus given great impetus by the initiative. Ostensibly the style was based on the architecture produced during the reign of Queen Anne (1701–14); in practice it was an eclectic style incorporating classical, Flemish and Renaissance influences.

When Sunderland School Board came into being it calculated that there were about 12,000 children of school age and that about half of them were already in education. It therefore needed to build six schools for 1,000 children each in order to meet its goals. It decided not to appoint an architect to design its buildings as many other boards did, but instead held a competition. This was derided by the professional press as it did not have an assessor, offered very small premiums and required the winning plan to become the absolute property of the Board without any promise to employ the successful architect. The real complaint, as expressed in a letter after the school was built, was that while two fellows of the RIBA were placed second and third, the winner was an auctioneer and brick maker.[78] The much-condemned winner was G.A. Middlemiss who, while he did lack formal architectural qualifications, had a track record of designing schools and devoted much time to his design, especially in respect of the ventilation systems, which were praised.

*James Williams Street Board School was built to Middlemiss's designs and opened in 1874 [Fig 35]. It was a single-storey building with pointed gables breaking out along the main axis and flèches over the ventilation shafts. As was typical of Board School designs, it was built of brick with stone dressings, and had separate entrances for boys and girls. It was based on an E-shaped plan, which provided 1,050 places at the reasonable cost of £6 per head.[79] Internally, the school had very high ceilings, allowing the circulation of air. As a result of this design, Middlemiss was asked to build the next five schools up to 1878, by which time he had virtually retired from architecture apart from some estate designs. He used his basic plan, adapting it to the sites, to build *Numbers Garth School (1874), *Thomas Street School (1876), *Garden Street School (1876), *Moor School, Chapel Street (1877) and *Diamond Hall School (1878). Effectively, Middlemiss had become architect to the School Board.[80] After this initial period of activity the Board built new schools, only to meet increased demand for places as the town grew. They continued to use competitions, which were routinely criticised for deviating from best practice, but a range of well-established architects won commissions. The constraints of cost tended to make the designs rather similar, though J.W. Rounthwaite (1852–1927) did manage a more striking job of Simpson Street School in 1884, where the steep drop in the site made a forbidding frontage to the street, relieved by an octagonal return at the top of the hill with a turret to mark it out[81] [Fig 36].

The Newcastle architects Oliver and Leeson also won school commissions, including *Chester Road School in 1895. Because it had a smaller site, this was

35 James Williams Street Board School by G.A. Middlemiss, 1874. (Image courtesy of Sunderland Museum)

36 Simpson Street School by J.W. Rounthwaite, 1884.

more like the schools built in London by E.R. Robson. Four corner stairways
gave access to the various floors and to a flat roof that doubled as an exercise
yard.[82] Oliver and Leeson also won the competition for the most prestigious
school in the system: ★West Park Higher Grade School, Cowan Terrace, later
known as Bede Collegiate Schools. This school enabled selected pupils to stay
on after the leaving age of fourteen to prepare for college, and in particular to
become teachers in Board Schools. Oliver and Leeson were becoming specialists
in this sort of school and built several in the region – at Hexham, Durham,
Newcastle and Gateshead. Cowan Terrace was built in brick and had ornamental
gables.[83] When the School Board was replaced by the council, competitions were
more commonly limited to local architects. A competition for a new school in
Waverley Terrace, Pallion, was won by Vaux and Mark in 1907. Oliver Hall
Mark (b.1877) was to become the architect to the Education Committee from
about 1919 and therefore did most of their designing until about 1947.[84]

   As well as elementary schools, provision was made for other types
of education. There had been an Art School in the town for some time,
for several years located on the upper floor of the Town Hall. Similarly,
the need for technical education in a shipbuilding and engineering town was
recognised, and eventually a dedicated building was erected. The council
gave its approval for such an institution in 1894, and a site on Green Terrace
was purchased in 1896. This had previously been occupied by Southgate

House, a plain building that had been used as a private school. The college was built under powers granted to local authorities by the Local Taxation (Customs and Excise) Act of 1890 to draw on central funds for technical education. Effectively this meant that the building was funded by the receipts from taxes on alcohol, which the Corporation had saved over a number of years.[85] The shipbuilder R.A. Bartram had donated funds to Sunderland Town Council and these were also used to build the college. Bartram was later knighted in recognition of his philanthropy, which also included funding St George's Presbyterian Church.

The Technical College was built in 1899–1901, after a competition in which all the premium winners were from outside the region [Fig 37]. The winner was the firm of Potts, Son and Hennings of London and Manchester, who had made their reputation designing technical innovations for cotton spinning mills and building many Nonconformist chapels. A.W. Hennings (*c*.1857–1926) was now in charge of the firm and was trying to move the practice into new areas. He produced a building in red brick encrusted with terracotta details. While essentially practical, the building had a grand façade in an English Renaissance style. On the main elevation two projecting sections balance each other under wide ogee pediments. A stolid but decorous tower rises at the corner, with heavily rusticated arches at the base. The tower is crowned by the dome of an observatory for navigational studies. This unique feature makes the building's

37 The former Technical College in Green Terrace by Potts, Son and Hennings, 1899–1901.

38 Terracotta emblem representing the discipline of mechanical engineering.

original purpose unmistakable: from here the pupils could monitor shipping traffic in and out of the port. A cupola sits astride the roof, where its function was to ventilate the building. Alongside the tower, the porch has a swan-necked pediment with vivid nautical symbolism. Figures of mermaids brandish an escutcheon emblazoned with the arms of Sunderland Borough, and a globe of the earth indicates that the college trained pupils for careers as seafarers and marine engineers. Emblems of chemistry and mechanical engineering testify to other subjects taught at the college [Fig 38]. All of this ornamentation was executed in terracotta, a relatively inexpensive material that was ideal for decorative and symbolic details. It was frequently used by public buildings such as schools and colleges to declare their social missions. With its fiery colour and institutional appearance, the college resembles the red brick and terracotta Board Schools built in accordance with the Elementary Education Act of 1870.

As with many public buildings of the period, the decorous façade masks an innovative structure: the building has concrete floors and steel reinforcement. The laboratories had very high ceilings to allow the circulation of air and the wide corridors and stairways made use of much tile work. The Technical College was Sunderland's most prestigious educational institution. Its first principal was Benchara Bradford, who was appointed with a salary of £500 per annum. The four departments were Chemistry, Mechanical and Civil Engineering, Physics and Electrical Engineering, and Commerce and Languages. Part-time lecturers taught additional subjects, including naval architecture, navigation and Latin. When the college opened in 1901, 671 students enrolled, more than three times the number expected.[86]

3

Ecclesiastical Buildings

As Sunderland's population grew, attention turned to providing all the facilities that the town would need. Some of these requirements were well established, such as the provision of shops, markets and places to conduct business, though these responded to changes in technology and public expectations. Others were entirely new building types, such as waterworks and gas works. Transport facilities like railways and tramways were needed, along with specialist office buildings. However, the buildings that architects were particularly eager to design were churches because their larger budgets gave architects larger fees, while the clients' aspiration to make an impact on the townscape gave greater scope for architectural display. These were the buildings which made a man's reputation. Equally, these were the buildings that generated debate within the profession about the most appropriate styles. The most famous and bitter of these debates was led by men like A.W.N. Pugin (1812–52), who argued that the revival of medieval Gothic forms was the most appropriate style in which to build churches and ultimately even Nonconformist chapels. The Gothic style also came to be used for building types that had no medieval precedents from which to draw inspiration. Although few of the leading architects of the nineteenth century came to design buildings in the town, these debates were reflected in the work of local and regional architects who built the townscape of Sunderland.

Anglican Churches

All denominations found that they needed new churches to provide for the growing population. This pressure was increased when the Religious Census of 1851 showed that less than half the people of Sunderland attended church on census day, and that if they had all wished to come to worship very many would have found there was no pew available for them. For the Church of England the problem was exacerbated by their claim to be a Church for everyone in the community and by the discovery that in Sunderland the Nonconformists, and especially the Methodists, could claim to be outstripping the Anglicans in the numbers they attracted to worship. The figures showed that Anglicans could accommodate 14 per cent of the population of the town while the other denominations had room for 32.5 per cent; only 25 per cent of all worshippers on that Sunday were at the Church of England.[87] Whatever may have been the deeper reasons for non-attendance, it was clear that more churches were needed. In 1815 the Anglicans had only four churches to minister to the town; by 1915 they had thirty – of which several had schools attached and most had parish halls and parsonages. This represented a large commitment of effort and resources and provided many opportunities for architects. Most of the chosen architects were based in the town or in the region.

The first new buildings were chapels of ease, converted from a house in ★South Hylton (1817) and a simple chapel in Ryhope (1827), to end the long journeys to St Michael's Church, Bishopwearmouth, every Sunday. The first proper church was built to serve the middle-class residents of the new Fawcett Street area. ★St Thomas's Church was built in 1829 on the corner of John Street to designs by Philip Wyatt (d.1835), the least productive and most unreliable of the London-based Wyatt architectural family, who had a tendency to fall out with his clients.[88] He was working on Wynyard Hall at the time and Lord Londonderry was so unhappy with him that he would only communicate with Thomas Prosser, the clerk of works. This does not seem to have happened with St Thomas's Church. Wyatt produced a Gothic design that lacked any real knowledge of medieval churches, but this is not surprising as he was mainly influenced by French classical design.[89] This was the building that introduced the Gothic Revival to Sunderland, but that was probably because it was in part funded by a parliamentary grant and the commissioners felt that they got more sittings for their money using Gothic designs.

After this, the next churches were intended to provide accommodation for poorer areas of the town. ★St Andrew's Church, Deptford (1840–41), was designed by Thomas Moore. This was a Gothic design by an architect who was much happier working in the classical style, though he did provide 1,220 sittings for only £2,500.[90] John Dobson was the pre-eminent architect of Victorian Newcastle and like Moore was primarily a classicist, but he did design a number of Gothic churches throughout his career. Dobson designed two churches in Sunderland: All Saints', Fulwell Road (1846–49),[91] and ★St Paul's, Hendon (1852), where he also designed the ★rectory and ★school.[92] Both were plain buildings in the Early English style and neither represented his best work. All Saints' was built for the working-class residents of Monkwearmouth. At first glance, it seems to be a small, unremarkable parish church, but the building does have powerful architectural lines. The nave and side aisles are encompassed within a single broad gable, creating a plunging roofscape. Symmetry is offset by an octagonal tower and spire at the right. A low chancel projects along the main axis of the building

39 All Saints' Church, Fulwell Road, by John Dobson, 1846–49.

and the interior is illuminated by three plain lancets in place of a large east window. Strong clasped buttresses grip the corners of the building and all of the gables are surmounted by crosses [Fig 39].

St Michael and All Angels has been the parish church of Bishopwearmouth since the Middle Ages. The church crowns the crest of a slope, which is all that survives of Bishopwearmouth Green. The present church is the result of centuries of rebuilding. A stone church had been built in the thirteenth century and remnants of it survive in the present structure. The tower dates from 1807 and is Gothic in style, ending in battlemented parapets. The transepts were designed by John Dobson in the Decorated style (1849–50), but the main body of the church was designed in a conservative manner by W.D. Caröe (1933–35).[93] More striking is Holy Trinity, Southwick, largely because of its position on a hillside surrounded by an extensive churchyard. This was designed by George L. Jackson of Durham (1802–45) in 1842–43. Jackson was the son of a builder and was trained by Ignatius Bonomi before becoming clerk of works to Durham Cathedral. He designed several churches in mining villages in the diocese and they all tend to be similar. Holy Trinity, despite its Gothic detailing, is much like its namesake in Sunderland, with a symmetrically placed west tower and a simple rectangular plan.[94] The intricate tower is strengthened with polygonal buttresses, which rise to form obelisk pinnacles. Strong clasped buttresses rise at the corners of the building and end in pinnacles echoing those of the tower. A narrow chancel projects at the east end, its windows decorated with carved faces [Fig 40].

The interior has a queen-post roof on corbels and there is a gallery at the west end. The altar is of painted stone, with cusped panels containing paintings of the Evangelists. A chamfered arch leads to the chancel, where the floor is lined with tiles in a geometric pattern. An impressive array of stained glass commemorates important local families. Lancet windows in the chancel are dedicated to Agnes Collingwood (d.1875) and Sarah Thompson (d.1866). These represent Christ the Good Shepherd, as well as Faith and Hope, and were designed by Alex Gibbs of Bloomsbury, London. The south-east nave window is also signed by Gibbs and dedicated to Collingwood, a former rector (d.1898). Another window on the north depicting the Good Samaritan is dedicated to Charles Pickersgill, owner of the Crown Road shipyard.

After 1851 the pressure to build grew stronger, and there emerged a number of architects who had been trained within a Gothic Revival tradition and possessed good archaeological knowledge of medieval architecture. Some of them devoted virtually their entire careers to designing and restoring churches, and they became strong protagonists of particular Gothic styles. This process was encouraged by clergymen influenced by the Oxford Movement, which aimed to revive a liturgy based on the ancient rituals of the church. For them a fully medieval building was necessary to achieve their spiritual goals. The debate about the proper form of church design and worship within these buildings was heated and at times bitter.

40 Holy Trinity Church, Southwick, by George L. Jackson, 1842–43.

This more informed use of medieval forms is exemplified by Christ
Church in Mowbray Road (1862–65) [Fig 41]. The design was the result of
a competition held in 1862, which was won by the young Coventry architect
James Murray (1831–63). Murray trained in Liverpool and had been a partner
of E.W. Pugin (1834–75), the son of the most zealous exponent of the Gothic
Revival, A.W.N. Pugin. He was, therefore, fully conversant with the
requirements of Gothic design. Unfortunately, Murray never saw the building
completed; he died during construction and his former assistant, John Cundall
(1830–89) of Leamington Spa, took over the supervision.[95] The volumes are
clutched low to the ground and hooded beneath steeply pitched roofs that
ascend one from another to culminate in a solid tower and broach spire.
The rugged, muscular massing is complemented by the material, a rock-faced
limestone dressed with minimal amounts of ashlar. Aisles rise to the base of
a low clerestory, where the rough but richly textured walls are punctured by
small roundel windows. The sharp ridge of the nave is bisected by powerful
transepts, making the north-south axis almost as prominent as the traditional
east-west axis. A wide porch is slung against the north aisle. The tower is
strengthened by corner buttresses with gargoyles projecting from the vertices
and niches articulating the multifaceted spire. Although the church is
conducted in a rustic spirit with snecked stonework, its sculpture is extremely
rich. The emblems of the Evangelists appear on the faces of the tower and

41 Christ Church, Mowbray Road, by James Murray, 1862–65.

vigorous naturalistic carving abounds. The interior unfolds with typical High Victorian splendour, divided into nave and side aisles by Gothic arcades with marble piers and stiff-leaf capitals. Geometric tracery occurs in the fine east window, which originally encapsulated a bright array of stained glass by the influential firm of Morris and Co. (1864).[96] The vivid scenes were designed by William Morris himself and the Pre-Raphaelite painter Sir Edward Burne-Jones (1833–98). The window was probably a result of the influence of local glass magnate James Hartley, who gave most of the money to build the church.

The total cost of the church amounted to £7,000. The prominent site was sold by the Quaker banker, Edward Backhouse, whose only proviso was that the church be given a good spire. Accordingly the tower was placed at the north-east corner, rising assertively to give prominence to the building. The design therefore represents a break from the symmetrical churches that had been seen in the town up to this time. Christ Church was the first fully achieved Gothic Revival church in Sunderland. With its imaginative massing, rich texture and Arts and Crafts fittings, the building anticipated St Andrew's Church at Roker (1907).[97]

Canon Cockin, rector of Bishopwearmouth, made a concerted attempt to remedy the shortage of church sittings in the town in 1867 with the Bishopwearmouth Rectory Act. This allocated part of the revenues of St Michael's to supporting clergy in daughter churches. In so doing, Canon Cockin solved one of the most difficult problems in building new Anglican churches – creating districts from within existing parishes, which then reduced the stipends of existing incumbents. A total of £3,620 per annum was made available, of which £1,740 was to be used in four new parishes.[98] These churches all opened between 1872 and 1874 and were all designed by men from the region. ★St Peter's Church, Cumberland Street, was designed by G.A. Middlemiss. Middlemiss worshipped there and was churchwarden until he moved to Ashbrooke Tower. This was an Early English design with an apsidal east end and a tower with a short spire. The church was built so close to St Michael's that it was never likely to have a long life.[99] St Matthew's Church, Silksworth, was designed as more of a village church set in a churchyard. It served the new mining community in a distant part of St Michael's parish. John Henry (1815–93), who was clerk of works to Durham University, also opted for an Early English lancet style in stone, though with an east window with Decorated tracery.[100] There was a competition with an invited entry of local architects for St Mark's Church, Millfield, which was intended to serve the expanding area of housing around Hartley's Glassworks. James Hartley was chairman of the building committee and the principal benefactor. The competition was won by Joseph Potts and Son. Built in a modernised Gothic style, the exterior has rather heavy detail, though the stone-finished interior with its chancel apse is more impressive. St Mark's (1871–72) is a rugged

42 St Mark's Church, Millfield, by Joseph Potts and Son, 1871–72. The church was
built for the community surrounding Hartley's Glassworks.

building in snecked stone [Fig 42]. The church rises from wide, spreading
aisles and transepts. A porch runs across the frontage, braced with three
strong buttresses with twin doors set between. Each of the doors has
elaborate hinges and is framed by shafts with stiff-leaf capitals. The gable
is pierced with two lancet windows and a quatrefoil. A pointed arch is
formed in the stonework, enclosing the windows. The steeply pitched roof
is surmounted by a bellcote. As a low building, St Mark's has a very short
clerestory, and for this reason the clerestory windows overlap with the
roofscape as Gothic dormers. A low semicircular apse emerges at the east
end, braced with buttresses between lancet windows.

The interior is rather dark, but the fittings are finer than the exterior
suggests. Although the church itself is in the Early English style, the apse
features a reredos in Perpendicular Gothic style, with painted panels and
sharp finials. The apse is framed by an extremely plain pointed arch, like
those dividing the nave from the aisles. However, the round piers have richly
foliated capitals. The north porch has fine stained glass representing St George,
and the pulpit and Communion rail are enriched with brass and wrought
iron. The opening of the church, with a procession that included trumpets,
banners and a surpliced choir, drew criticism that the vicar was following
'Romish' practices, and this had to be rebutted by the churchwarden, Henry
Ritson, in a lecture and pamphlet entitled 'The Ritual of St Mark's', which
demonstrated that all elements of the church were within the rubrics of the

Anglican Church.[101] Nevertheless, the taint of Romish practice caused a stir in the town, and it has been suggested that a nearby railway station was daubed with graffiti reading 'Change here for Rome.'[102]

The most ambitious of the churches was St Luke's, Pallion, which was designed by J.P. Pritchett (1830–1911) of Darlington. Pritchett had a large general practice and, although raised as a Congregationalist and working extensively for Nonconformists, he designed a number of Anglican churches. Pritchett used French Gothic as his model, and with a rather larger budget than the other churches he was able to include a 120ft tower and spire (since demolished).[103] At about the same time both Potts and Pritchett built other churches in the town. In 1872–74 Potts designed St Margaret's Church, Castletown, in the Early English style. Built in brick, the church made a half-hearted attempt at polychromy, which was a fashion not widely used in the North East.[104] Pritchett again used French Gothic to design the ★Venerable Bede Church, Hedworth Place, Monkwearmouth (1868–70), which was planned with a tower, but only built with a flèche.[105] The chapel at Ryhope was also superseded in 1869–70 by the imposing church of St Paul designed by Thomas Ebdy (1839–1911), who practised briefly in Sunderland but was mainly based in Durham [Fig 43]. Ebdy was deliberately original in his adaptation of Gothic motifs, as was becoming the fashion among some architects who declined to simply follow medieval precedent. E.B. Lamb (1806–69) seems to have been a particular influence. The great south tower

43 St Paul's Church, Ryhope, by Thomas Ebdy, 1869–70.

with its stair turret and pyramidal roof, and the contrast of the rubble stone and freestone dressings, make St Paul's one of the most distinctive churches in the town.[106] In the decade 1864–74 the Church of England had added 4,032 sittings at a cost of £32,212, together with restorations of existing churches costing £11,203. With the provision of six organs and eight schools, the total expenditure was about £52,000.[107]

In the remaining years of the century new churches were largely built by the specialist church architects from the region. The most prolific of these was Charles Hodgson Fowler (1840–1910). The son of a Nottinghamshire rector, Fowler was trained by Sir George Gilbert Scott and came to Durham in 1864. He became clerk of works at Durham Cathedral and served the Chapter as architect from 1885 to his death. His practice was almost entirely based on the restoration and design of churches and their fittings in the North East and throughout the country. His designs were based on a good archaeological knowledge of medieval buildings, and so he was reliable and generally sensitive in his restoration work.[108] In Sunderland he built three new churches. After the chapel of ease at South Hylton was destroyed by fire he designed the new church of St Mary in 1879–80. This followed the usual Early English style, which was favoured in the diocese because it was relatively cheap, but Fowler included some more sumptuous fittings in the chancel, with an imposing reredos.[109] In 1889 Bishop Joseph Barber Lightfoot (1828–89) determined to build a church at his own expense in the neediest parish in the diocese to mark his tenth anniversary as bishop. Hendon was selected as the most worthy parish and the resultant church was St Ignatius the Martyr. The layout and fittings were planned by Lightfoot himself, who also chose the first rector, Edgar Boddington. Designed by Fowler, the church is a good example of inspiring High Victorian architecture and is surprisingly grand for a working-class parish[110] [Plate 3].

The *Building News* described the church as 'very severe outside, as the smoke of a large town and the nearness of the sea would soon affect elaborate work, so all the ornamentation has been reserved for the interior, but the exterior is a remarkably good piece of stonework'[111] [Fig 44]. A tower rises at the south-west corner, enlivened with moulded openings and a broach spire. The west face is pierced with tall lancets and an elliptical opening. The tall clerestory hints at the impressive scale within: the soaring interior culminates in a high altar raised on a dais of marble and backed with an elaborate reredos, an arrangement that followed advice from Bishop Lightfoot. Figurative sculpture is framed by delicate Perpendicular tracery. At the west end the octagonal font is decorated with emblems of the Evangelists. The west windows are dedicated to Bishop Lightfoot and consist of multiple panels depicting scenes from his life, thus forming a vast illuminated biography. One pane shows him preaching at St Paul's Cathedral in London, where he was a canon. Another depicts Lightfoot as the founder of St Ignatius's, holding a model of the church. The inscription reads 'What shall I render unto the Lord for his benefits toward me?' It is rare for Anglican churches to be dedicated to St Ignatius, but since Lightfoot had published commentaries on the Epistles of St Ignatius (in 1885) the dedication is appropriate here. Lightfoot consecrated the church on 2 July 1889. The total cost was around £7,500.

Fowler's other church, St Columba's in Southwick (1888–90), is much more unusual as it is modelled on the church of Santi Vincenzo e Anastasio alle Tre Fontane in Rome. St Columba's is a vast basilican church that rises above the ranked terraces of Southwick.

44 The interior of St Ignatius's Church, Hendon, as illustrated in *Building News*, 21 February 1890, p.270.

Funds were limited, and Fowler was obliged to build in brick rather than stone. Brick lent itself to the Romanesque style, which was cheaper to execute than Gothic and did not require intricate ornamentation. The brick construction gives the church a blunt, rugged dignity, as well as a symbolic connection to the surrounding houses. The vast bulk is divided into a broad nave and side aisles, supporting an extremely high clerestory. The powerful lines of the nave continue into the chancel, which ends with a semicircular apse with conical roof. Down the nave walls the bays are divided by shallow pillars. The frontage has porches running the full width of the building, but the bold form of an apsidal baptistery rises from the porches and terminates with another conical roof. The west face is a largely unbroken expanse of brick, but in true Romanesque fashion it is punctured with a colossal wheel window. The grouping of the church and campanile with its later schools by Frank Caws (1893) and clergy house is undeniably powerful [Fig 45].

The interior is equally impressive in its uncompromising severity. Arcades run down the full length of the nave, composed of plain Romanesque arches on round piers [Plate 4]. A rich communion rail is executed in cream, green and red marble. The chancel has a marble mosaic floor incorporating the local stone known as Frosterley Marble, in fact a Carboniferous limestone containing fossilised coral. There is also a square font in dark marble with Romanesque carving. The forms of the church are bold and monumental, but a note of richness was introduced by the artist James Eadie Reid (1856–1928), who painted a spectacular series of murals in 1899. The apse was painted with biblical scenes and images of early saints, including Columba, Cuthbert and Aidan. Reid's biblical images were inspired by

45 St Columba's Church, Southwick, by C. Hodgson Fowler, 1888–90.

visits to the Holy Land. Between 1900 and 1908, he designed stained glass for the Gateshead Stained Glass Company, and many of the windows at St Columba's are signed 'J.E.R. 1905'. Built in the working-class district of Southwick, St Columba's Church was intended to be a striking statement of the High Church ministry that flourished there.[112] The dedication to St Columba and the fact that the fabric incorporated Irish stone suggests an intention to unify Irish and Anglo-Saxon Christianity. It was probably the first vicar, William Bird Hornby, who determined the church's overall character, and it is possible that he suggested the style to Fowler.[113]

Robert James Johnson (1832–92) has been described as the best architect of his generation in the region and one whose reputation would have been much higher if he had moved from Newcastle to London. He had a general practice and was equally adept at using classical models in his commercial buildings as he was with Gothic for churches. Initially in partnership with Thomas Austin, with whom he purchased the practice of John Dobson, he was also later in partnership with W.S. Hicks, though for most of the time he designed all the work himself.[114] The most sensitive commission he received in Sunderland was the restoration of St Peter's Church, Monkwearmouth. Interest in the Saxon tower and concern for its preservation was growing in the nineteenth century, and in 1866 Johnson was asked to report on the condition of the church. His report was published in *The Ecclesiologist*. The outcome was the conservation of the Saxon remains and the building of virtually a complete new church for the use of parishioners. This was accomplished in 1875, following as far as possible the lines of the original foundations and what was known of the original church, though the result is thoroughly Victorian.[115] His other Sunderland churches were undistinguished: ★St Barnabas's, Hendon (1866–68), was a brick barn with a large wheel window[116] and ★St Stephen's, Ayres Quay (1878–79), was a plain town church also in brick.[117] Both churches were intended to provide more accommodation in working-class districts and were supported by local industrialists. St Stephen's Church was credited to Austin, Johnson and Hicks, but William Searle Hicks (1849–1902) was at that time running the office in Middlesbrough. He set up on his own in Newcastle in 1885 and specialised in ecclesiastical work. Like Fowler, he did much restoration and refurnishing as well as new churches, particularly for the new Diocese of Newcastle.[118] In Sunderland his only work was ★St Hilda's Church, Westbourne Road (1892–94), for which he won the competition with his partner and brother in law, H.C. Charlewood (1857–1943). This was a second competition as Henry Thomas Gradon (1855–1917), then of Alexander and Gradon of Middlesbrough, had been successful in 1888.[119] By this time Alexander had moved to South Africa; Gradon went out briefly to join him before returning to Durham. Their successful competition entry was built abroad but was not used in Sunderland.[120] Instead, W.S. Hicks built a simple lancet style rectangle with only a flèche to mark the chancel break externally, but with a rood screen to mark it internally. The internal height and the decorated chancel belied the plain exterior. It also had an unusual outdoor pulpit in the angle between the nave and transept. Like St Peter's Church, Cumberland Street, it was so close to St Michael's that it was not needed for very long, and was demolished to allow for extensions to Sunderland Polytechnic[121] [Fig 46].

The Edwardian period saw the need for new churches maintained as housing spread still further out. In 1909–10 All Saints' Church, Fulwell Road, sponsored a small daughter church to serve Roker. H.T.D. Hedley provided a red brick church with chancel, nave and an Italianate tower: this was St Aidan's

46 The interior of St Hilda's Church, Westbourne Road, as illustrated in *Building News*, 7 March 1890, p.340.

Church in St George's Terrace.[122] On the south of the town Grangetown was becoming too populous to be served by St Paul's Church, Ryhope, and so St Aidan's, Ryhope Road, was planned in 1908 to replace the mission room in Spelter Works Road [Fig 47]. Charles Hodgson Fowler's modest Gothic design was built of red brick with dressings of red sandstone. The church has a tripartite structure, broken to form a nave and side aisles beneath steeply pitched roofs. Perpendicular tracery hints at a higher degree of splendour within. The nave and aisles are divided by arches of red sandstone resting on octagonal piers and the capitals are 'brattished' or sculpted to resemble castle battlements. High-quality woodwork abounds, from panelled wainscotting to a communion rail and pulpit with Perpendicular carving. A choir extends before the chancel, defined by a low choir screen with linenfold panelling and oak choir stalls with gilded tracery. As is typical of tripartite churches, the chancel is not divided from the nave, but occupies the final two bays. The lady chapel has a particularly fine wooden screen and a triptych reredos depicting religious scenes in low relief; the central image is the Adoration of the Magi [Fig 48]. At the west end of the church is an octagonal font executed in red sandstone, carved with emblems of the Evangelists. Most of the windows are of clear glass, filling the interior with light, but the east windows have high-quality painted glass. The ceiling is studded with Tudor flowers. Hodgson Fowler died while the building was under construction, so the project was modified by his former

47 St Aidan's Church, Ryhope Road, by C. Hodgson Fowler, 1911.

48 Triptych reredos in the lady chapel of St Aidan's Church, Ryhope Road.

pupil W.H. Wood (1861–1941), who took over the practice in 1911.[123] The church was only fully completed in 1930, when the south aisle, chancel, sanctuary and vestries were added. The additions were built to Fowler's original designs and in matching materials, and were gifts from George and Dorothy Short.

This period saw the building of St Andrew's Church, Roker, in 1906–07, the finest building in Sunderland [Plate 6]. The church was built by the local shipbuilder Sir John Priestman as a memorial to his mother. Designed by the 'rogue architect' Edward Schroeder Prior (1852–1932), the church is built of reinforced concrete but clad in rugged local stone.[124] This produces a bold, almost primitive building of incredible expressive power. Prior was educated at Harrow and Cambridge before training in the office of Richard Norman Shaw (1831–1912), one of the most innovative architects of his generation. As much an academic as an architect, Prior was deeply familiar with medieval Gothic buildings and committed to ideals of individual expression by his craftsmen. Another priority was fidelity to materials, which Prior believed should be used wherever possible in a handcrafted way.

The church is sited close to the sea on cliffs and forms a solid base from which a robust tower rises to dominate the building and to provide a landmark to sailors. Although basically Gothic, the imposing masses are not refined into delicate forms but are left stark and blunt. This deliberate crudeness arises from the use of a coarse grained local stone which is unsuitable for decorative treatment. By extolling these properties, the forms of the church seem to evolve organically from the materials. The plan is cruciform, but the robust transepts shrug off perfect symmetry. Unusually, the tower is not placed above the crossing but sits astride the chancel, which itself punches through the tower and obtrudes at the east, where the gable supports a gaunt cross. This restless interlocking of forms pervades the design. There is no grand entrance, only two humble porches under lean-to roofs with stone slates. Inside the nave, arches double as internal buttresses, emerging immensely thick and heavy from the walls but tapering inwards to form vast transverse arches that vault across the entire space, creating a cavernous interior. The arches are abruptly cut off at head height and rest upon pairs of short hexagonal piers, creating tunnel-like passages beneath them. This innovative plan met Priestman's requirement that everyone should have a clear view of the altar, and contributed to the excellent acoustics that Priestman demanded for the organ [Fig 49].

Beneath the rugged stonework, the church conceals an innovative structure of reinforced concrete. The use of iron and concrete seems incompatible with the Arts and Crafts ideal of buildings that candidly express their construction, but it was typical of Prior to arrive at an individualistic interpretation of current principles. To his mind, reinforced concrete was 'only the simple straight forward elementary science of building'.[125]

Prior was true to his ideals of collaboration with craftsmen. Albert Randall Wells (1877–1942) was employed on site as resident architect, with authority to modify details in the design and to supervise the construction. Both he and Prior signed the plans. In selecting the stone, Prior avoided the mechanised

49 The interior of St Andrew's Church, Roker.

quarry at Fulwell in favour of a more distant quarry at Marsden, because this was still 'worked by quarrymen with their usual tool – the scutcher, a broad bladed pickaxe'.[126] The wood panelling was made in Priestman's shipyard and was deliberately irregular, using handmade nails. Leading members of the Arts and Crafts movement contributed fittings. The sculptor and typographer Eric Gill (1882–1940) created the lettering on the dedication panels, Randall Wells designed the font with its Celtic motifs on a wide stone bowl and the great furniture designer Ernest Gimson (1864–1919) made the exquisite lectern with mother of pearl and silver inlay, together with the crosses and candlesticks of wrought iron. The glass in the nave was made by hand to Prior's own recipe and shows streaks on its surface, so that the small panes throw scintillating light across the stonework and emphasise its coarse texture. The chancel is connected to the nave with arches that spring diagonally from the base of the tower and fuse it with the transepts, creating cave-like recesses for the organ and lady chapel. The chancel is hollowed out of the base of the tower and bursts with colour in the form of a mural designed by Prior in 1927 and executed by Macdonald Gill (1884–1947), brother of Eric. This is a pictorial retelling of Genesis, and the forms radiate from a central globe of alabaster representing the sun [Plate 5]. The Pre-Raphaelite painter Sir Edward Burne-Jones designed the tapestry that serves as a reredos; William Morris himself, the leader of the Arts and Crafts movement, designed the carpet that forms the flooring. This was coloured with vegetable dyes rather than the harsh chemical dyes typical of the period. Henry A. Payne (1868–1940) of Birmingham designed the stained glass in the chancel with an Ascension window, and in the lady chapel on the theme of earthly labour being rewarded in Heaven.

By combining enthusiasm for tradition and craftsmanship with new technologies like concrete, electric lighting and a heating and ventilation system worked by electric fans, Prior created an exceptional building with a breathtaking internal space. By using a resident architect and no general contractor he built it economically for about £10,000, and he provided Anglicans in Sunderland with a church of national importance.[127] Architecture and fittings combine to create a building internationally renowned as the Cathedral of the Arts and Crafts movement.

The need for a new church in the affluent district of High Barnes had become apparent by the early 1890s, prompting Robert Long, rector of Bishopwearmouth, to build a temporary corrugated-iron church in 1898. This was known as the 'tin tabernacle'. A more substantial stone mission church was built alongside and consecrated on 10 July 1901. St Gabriel's became a parish in its own right in 1904, and grew so swiftly that a fund was instituted for the building of a larger church to serve a parish of 10,000 souls. This led to a competition in 1908, judged by W.D. Caröe, who would rebuild St Michael's, Bishopwearmouth, in 1933–35. The competition was won by C.A. Clayton Greene, a Sunderland architect who was attuned to the latest developments

50 St Gabriel's Church by C.A. Clayton Greene, 1908–12.

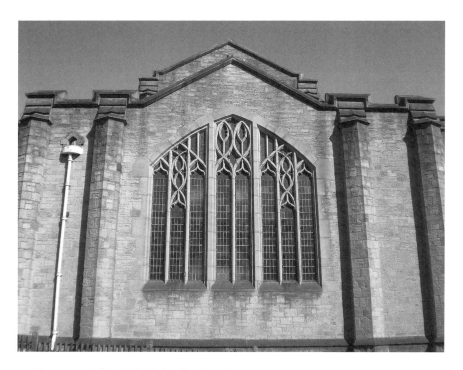

51 Transept window in St Gabriel's Church.

in progressive architectural circles[128] [Fig 50]. The church was built of snecked limestone in a neo-Tudor style, but the massing is highly inventive. An interplay of solid and void creates an almost abstract composition that makes effective use of stark, unbroken wall surfaces. The nave is tall and wide, with transepts cutting across the midpoint to give the impression of a square cross. Elaborating this form, the angles between nave and transepts are occupied by porches and octagonal stair turrets. The transepts are almost as tall as the nave, forming a very high crossing that was originally intended to support a tower. The gables rise through castellated battlements. Half-octagonal buttresses scale the blank transept walls, where large windows echo those of the nave. Wedged beneath the chancel is an undercroft. Here Greene used the slope of the ground to incorporate a hall and classrooms. The east face of the church is dominated by a vast window. Octagonal buttresses rise at the corners to form Tudor turrets decorated with blind tracery.

The internal layout was probably influenced by Prior's design for St Andrew's Church, Roker, in that the nave is a vast cavernous space and the large piers allow aisles to be formed beneath. Strong piers at the crossing of nave and transepts were built to support the proposed tower. The sanctuary is panelled with oak. The design of the church may be understood as an Art Nouveau interpretation of the Tudor style. The tracery is remarkably curvilinear and sinuous, resembling the flowing lines of Art Nouveau [Fig 51]. Greene had in fact travelled in Belgium, where he would have encountered Art Nouveau architecture first hand. Overall, the design is indicative of Edwardian architecture outgrowing the strictures of established styles such as Gothic, and moving into the realm of abstraction.

Roman Catholic Churches

Initially the problem for Roman Catholics was being able to build churches at all. Before the Catholic Emancipation Act of 1829 there were substantial restrictions on what Catholics could do, and their churches were often deliberately sited away from public view to avoid the risk of attack. This was true in Sunderland, where the *church and priest's house were in Dunning Street, having been built in 1786–88 to designs by William Wilkinson, a mason. They were subject to an arson attack before completion.[129] Immediately after the 1829 Act the Catholic community began to plan a new church, and took a site in Bridge Street on what would be the prime residential street in the town. Ignatius Bonomi was the architect. Based in Durham as county bridge surveyor, he had been trained by his father, who had migrated from Italy and developed a large practice in country houses. John Dobson recognised Ignatius Bonomi as the only other architect between York and Edinburgh, and his extensive works included several Catholic churches as well as country houses and official projects.[130]

St Mary's (1830–35) was only the second Gothic Revival church to be built
in Sunderland, and its rectangular floor plan and overall symmetry locate it
within the Georgian tradition [Fig 52]. Outwardly, however, the building
is a display of spirited medievalism. The frontage is rigidly symmetrical and
arrayed with pinnacles, niches and quatrefoils. A central pitch in the broad
tripartite façade alludes to the traditional Gothic gable, and three tall lancet
windows are lashed together within a vaulting pointed arch. Tall buttresses
are clasped to the surface, each accentuated by a sharp pinnacle. The naïve
use of Gothic forms is representative of the tentative beginnings of the
Gothic Revival. Inside, the box-like nave is illuminated by lancet windows
of clear glass. The flat ceiling is the antithesis of the soaring vaults typical
of medieval churches and the chancel, rather than being a separate space
enshrining the altar, is merely a shallow recess in the west wall. Nevertheless,
the chancel is furnished with an elaborate reredos replete with statues of
northern saints. There is no great window, but the reredos is flanked by
narrow stained-glass windows and the west wall is articulated with a
framework of Gothic decoration. Down the south wall are doors leading to
the confessionals; each terminates with a pointed arch containing sculptural
emblems. A macabre theme is introduced by the image of a skull wreathed
in creeping foliage. Typically for a Georgian church, there is a gallery at the
rear. Galleries fell into disrepute later in the nineteenth century, but were

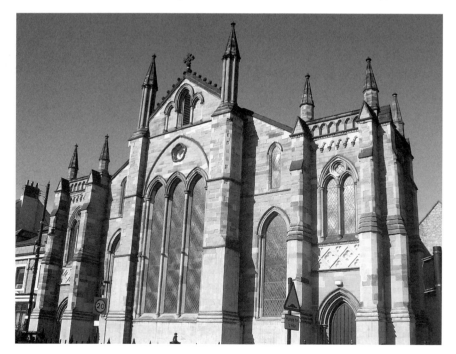

52 St Mary's Church by Ignatius Bonomi, 1830–35.

essential for accommodating the large congregations of the era, swelled by Irish migrants who flooded into northern industrial parishes.

St Mary's is grand for a Catholic church built so soon after the Catholic Emancipation Act. The exuberant design is a testament to the increasing tolerance and prosperity experienced by Catholics after legal restrictions on their faith had been lifted. This grandeur, however, is reserved for the façade. The frontage is of dressed stone, but the other walls were built of rough local limestone to reduce costs, and because the church was entirely bounded by other buildings, including priests' houses. Eventually the houses to the north were demolished, and this permitted the addition of a transept, which is linked to the nave by paired arches springing from a single column. Two original windows were filled in to make way for the transept arches, and their outlines are just visible on the north wall of the nave. Victorian architects would become more adept at using Gothic forms, but at this date the grammar of medieval architecture was not fully understood. Bonomi was primarily a classicist, and St Mary's is essentially a classical preaching box hidden behind a Gothic façade. The choice of style was significant, however. Gothic suggested continuity with the universal Catholic Church of the Middle Ages; St Mary's thereby provided a secure foundation for the resurgence of Catholicism in Sunderland. Contemporary opinion was favourable to the design, with the *Sunderland Herald* saying that '[it] will stand unrivalled as the finest public building in these towns'.[131]

St Mary's was intended for the traditional Catholic population of Sunderland, but like other industrial towns there was an influx of Irish workers and the Church needed to provide for them also. ★St Patrick's in Church Street (1860–61) was built to accommodate these immigrants. It was stone-built and had very tall lancets, but a combination of limited funds and a need for a large number of seats (1,000-plus) meant that it was practical rather than aesthetic. The building was designed by James Gillis Brown (1830–90), who was more of an engineer than an architect. He worked for the River Wear Commissioners under Thomas Meik and finally became assistant borough surveyor in 1880–88.[132] North of the river, St Benet's Church was built in 1888–89 [Fig 53]. This large red brick church in Decorated Gothic style replaced the school chapel that had served since 1867. The architects were the Newcastle firm of Dunn, Hansom and Dunn who were specialists in Catholic churches.

Archibald Matthias Dunn (1832–1917) was born in Wylam, the son of Matthias Dunn, a colliery inspector and member of a long-established Catholic family.[133] He was educated at the Catholic colleges of Ushaw and Stonyhurst, and received architectural training in the office of Charles Hansom (1816–88) of Bristol before returning to Newcastle to set up practice in 1854. Dunn went into partnership with Edward Joseph Hansom (1842–1900), the son and pupil of his former mentor. Under the style of Dunn and Hansom, the firm became the foremost Catholic architects in the North of England, and gained such notability from their church-building that they received three of the most prestigious Anglo-Catholic commissions since the Reformation – namely the colleges of Downside, Stonyhurst and Ushaw. A highlight of their career was designing the tower and spire of St Mary's Roman Catholic Cathedral in Newcastle (1871–72), which pierces the city's skyline. As Catholic architects based in the North of England, however, Dunn and Hansom were continually faced with the prospect of designing churches for the urban poor, which increasingly meant Irish migrant communities. The new churches were funded by public subscription, and while wealthy donors certainly made contributions, the main brunt of the cost was borne by working-class parishioners, who were among the poorest people in

53 Dunn, Hansom and Dunn's design for St Benet's Church, Causeway. This illustration shows that the church was intended to have a tower and spire, but these were never built. The image was published in *Building News*, 2 February 1883, p.126.

the North East. This is painfully evident in the number of small, aisleless churches that Dunn and Hansom produced throughout their career: devoid of decoration, they were little more than preaching boxes and were usually to be found in unenviable locations among gasworks, chemical works and factories. St Benet's Church was exemplary. Frugally executed in red brick, its most noteworthy feature is a statue of Benedict Biscop holding a model of the Saxon church he founded, St Peter's, Monkwearmouth. Illustrations in the *Building News* show that St Benet's was intended to have a tower, but the scheme was abandoned because of a lack of funds.[134]

St Benet's Church was served by Redemptorist Fathers, and in 1902 a monastery of bleak external appearance was built for twelve residents by Charles Walker, whose Newcastle practice was entirely confined to projects for the Catholics, including a design for St Benet's that was not built.[135] Another major architectural practice that specialised in Catholic buildings was that of George Goldie (1828–87), based in London. The patronage of Lady Beckwith of Silksworth House brought them to design St Leonard's Church, Silksworth, in 1872–73. In partnership with C.E. Child (1843–1911), Goldie produced a small apsed stone church in Early English style with a presbytery and school, which, like the Anglican church, suits its village location.[136]

St Joseph's Church, Millfield, began as a school chapel in 1873 in a building designed by James Charles Parsons (1841–1920), who was in practice in Newcastle from 1870 to 1910. By the turn of the century it needed to be replaced, and the present church was built in 1906–07 [Fig 54]. This is a unique structure in Sunderland as it was entirely built of concrete blocks made on site and moulded to suit their required location in the building. The external appearance is of rock-faced stone, and the style chosen was Romanesque with apsidal sanctuary and chapels. No attempt was made to disguise the method of construction. The internal columns were cast solid and ready carved, and no plastering was used within the building. The process had been invented by Thomas Axtell (d.1909), who was based in Ryhope and was clerk of works for the building of an extension to Ryhope Asylum in 1903. The parish priest, Father Rogers, helped to plan the church, and Axtell supervised the manufacture of the blocks, though he was credited as architect. Axtell was a founder member of the Concrete Institute in 1908, and it appears that his death prevented further exercises in a similar mode.[137] The only other Catholic churches built before the First World War were St Hilda's, Southwick (1908), in red sandstone and with rather coarse detailing by Theodor Korner (1885–1946), little known in England, but more active in Canada,[138] and St Patrick's, Ryhope, in 1914–15, a small brick church by an unknown architect.[139] There was much more building of churches and schools after 1945 as the new council estates drew people away from the old central districts.

54 St Joseph's Church, Millfield, by Thomas Axtell and the parish priest, Father Rogers, 1906–07.

The Catholic community also supported orders of nuns, especially to teach in their schools. A convent was acquired in Green Street, behind St Mary's, for the Sisters of Mercy in 1843. In 1909 they moved the school to Oaklea in Thornhill and W. and T.R. Milburn built a new convent for them in 1915. In 1900 the Milburns built the Holy Cross Home, and extended it in 1907–08. Maintained by the Little Sisters of the Poor, it stands on the site of High Barnes House – a gaunt red brick pile that is prominent in views in the south east of the town.[140]

Nonconformist Chapels

The many strands within Nonconformity all built extensively in the town in the nineteenth century, though most of the chapels were small, cheap and architecturally uninteresting. Many have subsequently been demolished or converted to secular uses. Old Dissent had built some chapels in the eighteenth century, and these followed the then established classical styles, often very plainly used, with the goal of enabling the largest number of people to hear the preacher as clearly as possible. The impact of the preaching visits of John Wesley (1703–91) led to the growth of Methodist societies, and they soon began to build meeting places for their Bible classes and services. Under Wesley's influence they also built in a simple classical style, placing greater emphasis on the practicality of the building than on its aesthetic appeal – in Wesley's words, 'neat, but not fine'. A ★chapel in Sans Street represented that tradition. This was built in 1793 by an unknown architect, though Bartholomew Dowell may have been involved, and extended in 1809 and 1824. The main long façade was domestic in appearance, with the three central bays brought forward under a pediment that contained the chapel's name and date. Access was by a central door, with side doors giving access to the galleries, which enabled the final accommodation to be for 2,000 hearers.[141] The chapel reputedly cost at least £5,000 to build, and this substantial sum was raised by selling shares to affluent members with the promise that they would receive interest in due course.

In the early years of the nineteenth century most of the denominations established at least one major chapel, often at severe financial pressure to the societies. The Methodist New Connexion opened ★Zion Chapel in Zion Street in 1809.[142] This was a classical preaching box with two tiers of round-headed windows between stark giant pilasters. The building terminated with a triangular pediment bearing the name and date of the building. The Baptists built in ★Barclay Street in 1813 and replaced that building in 1834.[143] The Society of Friends built a large meeting house in ★Nile Street in 1822, replacing an excessively plain building on High Street (1688), which had three square windows in the upper floor and a panelled door at the right.[144] The Primitive Methodists opened a chapel in ★Flag Lane in 1824, after repeated delays in construction while further funds were found.

This building hosted their national conference on five occasions.[145] All of these buildings adhered to eighteenth-century patterns of design, and their architects have not come down to us. Other denominations have recorded their architects. The classical ★Bethel Chapel in Villiers Street was built in 1818 by the Independents. It was designed by James Hogg (1785–1838), who was the son of James Hogg (d.1816), an auctioneer, joiner and estate owner who left £4,000 in his will.[146] In 1816 Hogg announced that as well as continuing his father's building business he would practise architecture, after several years' experience in Oxford and London.[147] He may well have been the first architect in Sunderland, as he is the only architect listed in the earliest directory for the town. He lived in Tatham Street, never married and died on 9 February 1838.

Bethel Chapel was a chaste white edifice with a five-bay façade of rendered rubble beneath a triangular pediment. The central bay was slightly recessed and the door was placed below a segmental window. Beneath the pediment the two outer bays were expressed as extraordinarily broad pilasters. The date 1817 was displayed on the pediment. The chapel cost around £3,000 to build, which was comparable to the other chapels in the vicinity – St George's and Bethesda. Sited on Villiers Street, the chapel indicates that Nonconformity was migrating from old Sunderland and making inroads into the more prestigious streets being built on the edge of Bishopwearmouth. The building was altered in 1826 and finally demolished in 1979.

Hogg also designed St George's Presbyterian Church, Villiers Street, in 1825. This was a much grander building of ashlar stone and with fine classical proportions, which denoted the status of the Presbyterians within the town.[148] St George's is a bold and confident design of striking austerity [Fig 55]. The ground floor has rusticated stonework, which gives an impression of strength and impregnability. The façade is dominated by a triangular pediment, supported on bold Doric pilasters. These are the basic elements of classical architecture and give the church the stern dignity of a Greek temple. In a break from strict classical formulae, however, the pilasters are not equidistant: the central bay is wider than the others, framing a panelled door. The heavy pediment displays the Roman numerals MDCCCXXV – 1825. There is evidence of further lettering, but this has been removed. Aside from the façade, the building is executed in coarse stone, although the rear has dressings of ashlar and a shallow apse. The church is set back from the street and bounded by railings, which were added in 1873. Standing alongside is the former school for St George's, a symmetrical two-storey building of 1849. The central door is framed by Tuscan columns and a severe entablature. Quoins reinforce the corners, and the building has a crowning entablature with a wide cornice.

On the north side of the river the Presbyterians used John Dobson to build their chapel in North Bridge Street (1827).[149] Known as the ★Scotch Church, this was a two-storey building in a severe classical style. The configuration of the frontage was very similar to the Exchange Building, with round-headed

55 St George's Presbyterian Church, Villiers Street, by James Hogg, 1825.

arches on the ground floor and projecting outer wings. These were defined by extremely tall pilasters supporting stark triangular pediments. Even when working with a small budget, Dobson was able to create dignified buildings by using the fundamental elements of classical architecture [Fig 56].

In the midst of all this chapel-building one project stood out. In 1836 the Wesleyans opened ★Fawcett Street Chapel right at the heart of the most fashionable area in town [Fig 57]. The building committee had decided to use a fashionable style of architecture. Although the chapel

56 The Scotch Church, North Bridge Street, by John Dobson, 1827. (Image courtesy of Sunderland Museum)

was fitted onto two house-building sites within the terrace and was directly abutted by houses, the external details were in the Gothic style. The entrance was defined by an arcade of small pointed arches, below a large window with tracery. A castellated parapet ran along the roofline and a pointed gable rose at the centre. Four half-octagonal buttresses scaled the façade and terminated in crocketted pinnacles. The interior was also decorated in the Gothic style, but had an oval-shaped gallery all around. A hexagonal pulpit was raised on a pedestal and behind it was an organ with Gothic panelling. The chapel accommodated 1,450 people and was built at a cost of about £4,000. This was not authentic Gothic, as the building was a simple parallelogram in plan and the medieval decoration was applied to a basically classical design. Nevertheless, the use of a medieval and Catholic style of architecture for a Nonconformist chapel was controversial and was vigorously debated nationally, though in Sunderland the controversy centred on the introduction of an organ to replace the variety of instruments used hitherto. In its architecture and location the chapel was probably a riposte to the Catholics, who had recently built the prominent church of St Mary on Bridge Street. The architect was Joseph Potts (1799–1885), for whom this was a most important building, marking his move from mason and builder to architect. The Fawcett Street Chapel was the first Gothic Revival building in Sunderland designed by an architect from the town. Potts's daughter made an embroidered sampler of the façade, now in Sunderland Museum, which suggests that the building was seen as important within the Potts family.

Joseph Potts was born in Whickham but spent most of his life in Sunderland. He began as a builder and, although he founded an architectural practice, is described in the census of 1871 and 1881 as a retired builder or mason. He received no formal training in architecture and never joined any professional body. He retired from the firm in 1870 in favour of his son, Joseph Potts Jr, who was born in Sunderland on 2 May 1836. He joined his father in partnership when he was twenty-two and presumably learned his trade from him, but he never sought any formal qualifications as an architect. Most significantly he brought Frank Caws to Sunderland as a senior assistant. Potts maintained the firm as a local practice, though when his sons Henry and Charles joined him he opened an office in Newcastle and moved there in about 1890. The practice continued to the 1950s as J. Potts and Son.[150]

57 Fawcett Street Wesleyan Chapel by Joseph Potts, 1836. (Image courtesy of Sunderland Antiquarian Society)

Although the Fawcett Street Chapel did not bring an end to the use of classical designs, it did indicate that increasingly such designs would seem out of date. Thomas Moore, who was seen as the father of architecture in Sunderland and who was the only Sunderland-based architect to help found the Northern Architectural Association in 1859, designed a *classical chapel for the Unitarians in Bridge Street in 1830. Shops were included on the ground floor to help defray the costs.[151] The design was a provincial example of Greek Revival architecture. The chapel was built of white brick rather than stone, but the entrance had Doric columns *in antis* (indented into the façade). The windows too had Grecian frames. Moore went on to design more substantial classical buildings, the pinnacle of his career being Monkwearmouth station.

In 1840 Moore built a large chapel for the Primitive Methodists in *Williamson Terrace in brick and stone, which with its domestic sash windows looked more like a bank than a chapel.[152] In 1851 the congregation from Bethel moved to Fawcett Street into the *Ebenezer Chapel, designed by the Revd R.W. McAll (1821–93) and Thomas Oliver. It must have been more the work of McAll as the result was a coarse, ill-proportioned and completely incorrect collection of classical motifs [Fig 58]. A rusticated arch dominated the façade, overlapping awkwardly with a triangular pediment. The entrance was defined by a shallow portico with a segmental pediment. Stone quoins at the corners merely emphasised the poor composition. An obituary described McAll as 'an excellent architect and a good draughtsman', but this observation seems overly charitable, judging by surviving images of the building. Thomas Oliver, however, had shown how well he could handle classical designs in

58 Ebenezer Chapel, Fawcett Street, by the Revd R.W. McAll and Thomas Oliver, 1851. (Image courtesy of Sunderland Antiquarian Society)

the Londonderry Institute in Seaham (1853–55). He was also a winner in the 1853 Congregational Church Building Society competition that sought model designs for chapels that could be adapted to individual sites. The Fawcett Street chapel cannot possibly have been the basis for his successful entry.[153]

Another notable chapel is the Bethesda Free Chapel on Tatham Street, a modest Neoclassical building in plain brick. This chapel owes its existence to the 'Welsh firebrand' Arthur Augustus Rees (c.1815–84), a former Church of England curate. Rees was a charismatic preacher, but alienated the Bishop of Durham because of his Calvinistic tendencies and overly assertive personality. He was dismissed from his position as curate of Holy Trinity, Sunderland, and, failing to find another place in the Anglican Church, founded the independent Bethesda Free Chapel in 1844, funding the building out of his own pocket [Fig 59]. The site was purchased from Cable Wilson, a member of a local Quaker family. Architecturally, the building closely resembles St George's Presbyterian Church, with bays projecting under a triangular pediment. The name Bethesda Free Chapel appears on a large panel and the date 1844 is displayed on the pediment. Architectural adornment is reserved for the entrance, where a cornice projects on scrolled brackets. The frontage is built of simple brick; the sides are of limestone rubble and the rear elevation has dressings of ashlar. All of the windows have segmental stone lintels. Rees never described himself as a Baptist, but he was converted to a belief in adult baptism by immersion.[154] He was re-baptised in 1849 and introduced the practice at Bethesda, for which purpose a large baptismal pool was installed in the interior. Large congregations were drawn by Rees's oratorical powers, and by 1852 galleries had to be installed in the chapel, supported on fluted iron columns.

After the Religious Census of 1851 there was a quickening of building activity in all denominations, with 135 chapels being built or extensively improved by 1914 – an average of just over two per year. Most were small brick boxes with Gothic or, less commonly, classical details under a steeply pitched roof, with the gable making the main façade. They were generally designed by a local architect. Some have value in the townscape despite the limited budgets available, such as Franklin Street United Methodist Chapel facing Hylton Road. This was designed by Potts and Son in 1865.[155]

59 Bethesda Free Chapel, Tatham Street, 1844.

Chapels, especially for the United Methodist Free Church, became an important element in the firm's output when Joseph Potts Jr was in charge, even though these were mainly small chapels of little architectural pretension. The chapel in Franklin Street is a good example of the simple but effective use of basic materials in a typically Nonconformist style. Another example is the rather charming Hood Street United Methodist Chapel of 1867, in which John Tillman used white brick and large round arches in red brick to hold the design together.[156] Some architects came to specialise in chapel-building. The Tillmans designed at least twenty chapels for several denominations in the town between 1860 and 1875.[157] Potts and Son carried out ten projects for the United Methodists over a thirty year period.[158] John Eltringham built thirteen chapels from 1876 to 1905, and adopted a standard design in several of them: a central door under a four- or five-light window with a spirelet on the outside corner of the frontage.[159] Eltringham was the son of Stephen Eltringham (1818–94) from Corbridge, who took over a grocery shop in Roker Avenue in 1839. There is no information about John's education or architectural training, but he began practice in the town by 1881. He did not join any professional body and his only known pupil was F.E. Coates. It is probable that he spent his entire professional life in Sunderland; the practice was entirely local in scope and general in character. He was given several jobs by the Infirmary, but his most public commission was to extend the Victoria Hall, where he had to fit in with the existing design. Overall he offers little more than competence, and few of his buildings created much impact.

Among all this routine building to meet the need for more accommodation there were some attempts at more substantial and impressive chapels. This was particularly true when older buildings needed replacing because they were too small or no longer convenient for the wealthier members to attend. Most of these grand chapels are to be found in the more middle-class areas of town, with a particularly fine collection in Ashbrooke. The desire to replace an outdated chapel is demonstrated by the rebuilding of ★Williamson Terrace Primitive Methodist Chapel in 1881. Moore's classical building, only forty years old, was replaced by a brick chapel in Romanesque style (now also demolished) by Joseph Shields (1853–95), who was the son of a Primitive Methodist minister. Immensely tall, with a three-storey Norman arch rising to the gable over a double doorway and with three transverse gables on each side of the building, it was intended to make a statement about the enhanced status of chapel folk.[160] The Primitive Methodists attempted the same when they sought to leave Flag Lane for a new circuit centre in the brick Lombardic Gothic chapel in Tatham Street (1875) by J. and T. Tillman. The design was heavy and represented many of the worst elements of Victorian chapel architecture. The cost of the building, the provision of manses and the abandonment of such an important chapel in a poor area of town led many members to leave the society to form the Christian Lay Church, which operated without a full-time ministry. The desire for a new building had unintended consequences that damaged the denomination for many years.[161]

Other denominations achieved a move to more salubrious locations without the upheavals of the Primitives. Ebenezer Congregational Chapel in Fawcett Street was sold for commercial redevelopment and the money was invested in Grange Chapel, Cowan Terrace, opened in 1883. Here J.P. Pritchett of Darlington provided a remarkable church with a horseshoe of Sunday Schools [Fig 60]. These were built before the chapel and accommodated 600 scholars. The chapel was designed in the style of the late fourteenth century. It is built of rock-faced stone, but boasts an ashlar plinth and shafts of red granite, which add flashes of colour to the rugged façade. The west face has doors in the nave, tower and porch, all enclosed within projecting gables. Steps lead up to the highly placed west door, where the cast-iron hinges coil like tendrils. A tall west window with Geometric tracery illuminates the nave. The surging tower has paired lancets and clock-faces. An octagonal spire with fish-scale decoration rises from between obelisk spirelets. Double transepts cut across the nave, producing a traditional cruciform plan; however, a number of distinctive features raise the chapel above the conventional. The tower and porch both have octagonal stair turrets leading to internal galleries. The chapel's most remarkable feature is the sweeping bank of school rooms at the east end, forming a vast polygonal ambulatory. This layout was influenced by American examples Pritchett had studied before undertaking the commission.[162]

60 Grange Chapel, Cowan Terrace, by J.P. Pritchett, 1883.

Inside, the chapel has a dramatic hammerbeam roof coming to rest on short red granite piers and corbels. In common with many Nonconformist chapels in Sunderland, a gallery sweeps around three sides of the building. This is supported by two tiers of slender cast-iron piers whose crocketed capitals feature carved thistles. The plinths of the upper piers are painted with passion flowers and the names of virtues such as 'Brotherly Love' and 'Charity'. Occupying the focal point of the chapel is a pulpit of fine ashlar stone, with shafts of red and green marble and decorative carving in the style of Northern Italy. Deacons' seats are clustered around the pulpit. Behind the pulpit, the chancel arch is occupied by a fine Renaissance-style organ manufactured by Nelson and Co. of Durham.

The windows have high-quality painted glass. Two windows in the north gallery were salvaged from the Ebenezer Chapel on Fawcett Street. The large west window is dated 1902 and depicts Christ in Glory. The window in the north transept is signed by Atkinson Brothers of Newcastle and depicts the Sermon on the Mount and Christ's Charge to Peter and John. A small window in the north aisle was designed by James Eadie Reed and is one of his last works, dated 1926. Most significantly, there is a memorial window to the Revd Robert Whitaker McAll, a former Congregational minister at the Bethel Chapel on Villiers Street and founder of the Ebenezer Chapel on Fawcett Street. This window is located under the west gallery and can only been seen when the west doors are open: the sudden effect of light streaming through the window to illuminate the imagery is striking and brings to mind the Biblical command, 'Let there be light.' The window was unveiled by McAll's widow on 20 March 1898.[163] At the east end of the chapel the school rooms inside the ambulatory have Gothic details, including cast-iron piers with octagonal bases and fluted capitals.

The Methodist New Connexion left Zion Street for Park Road in 1887. John Eltringham's design was an improvement on his usual style because he had a larger budget to provide a full range of ancillary facilities and a more attractive site on which to work.[164] St George's Presbyterian Church moved to Belvedere Road in 1890 to a church designed by John Bennie Wilson of Glasgow (1849–1923), an experienced architect of churches in Scotland [Fig 61]. Wilson had designed the Crescent Church on Linenhall Street, Belfast (1885), which St George's Building Committee admired, and for this reason they asked him to produce a similar design.[165] The church was built in the affluent suburb of Ashbrooke and funded by the shipbuilder Robert Appleby Bartram (1835–1925), whose munificence accounts for the richness of the architecture and fittings. Wilson's robust Gothic design contrasts with the Neoclassicism of the earlier church. He used red sandstone from Dumfries in his native Scotland and much of the stonework is rock-faced, giving the church a rugged quality. Bartram himself laid the foundation stone on 7 February 1889.

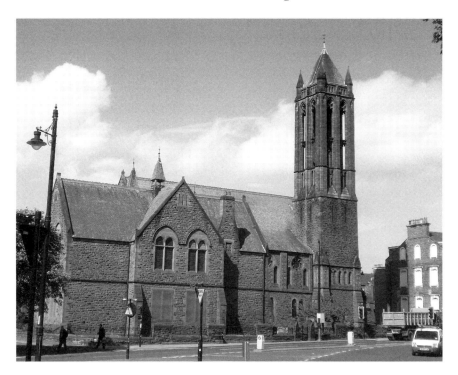

61 St George's Presbyterian Church, Belvedere Road, by John Bennie Wilson, 1890.

St George's was designed in the Early English style of the thirteenth century, which can be recognised by the use of plain lancet windows. The massing is bold and distinctive, in that the nave has extremely high side aisles to accommodate internal galleries, a standard feature of Nonconformist churches and chapels. The walls of the galleries are pierced by unusual windows, consisting of a roundel between lancet openings. Transepts project from the east end of the nave and a tower rises at the south-west corner. The church is an important landmark thanks to this highly original tower, which has an immensely tall belfry stage pierced with soaring lancets, leaving it open to the elements. In contrast to the rest of the building, the tower is constructed of crisply dressed stone. At its base is a gabled porch with richly carved foliage and short gabled buttresses. The tower ends with pinnacles and a squat pyramidal roof. This unusual tower in fact has a twin: Wilson's earlier church in Belfast boasts an identical structure.

The spaces within the building are vastly different from Anglican and Catholic churches of the period [Fig 62]. Conventionally, the nave and side aisles would be divided by arches and stone piers; at St George's, however, the aisles rise to the full height of the nave in order to accommodate galleries. These are supported on extremely slender cast-iron piers, creating an unimpeded flow of space. Rather than being set to one side,

62 Interior of St George's Presbyterian Church.

the pulpit occupies a central position, declaring the primacy of the Word in Presbyterian worship. In contrast to more conventional churches there is no chancel. Instead, the soaring Gothic arch at the east end is occupied by the church organ. The interior is austere and unpretentious, as one would expect from a Presbyterian church, but many of the fittings are of high quality. An ornate pulpit was added in 1907. The stained glass windows are richly coloured throughout, and one is dedicated to Bartram's only daughter, M.A. Thompson (1865–1906). Chairs and a conference table for the elders of the parish are placed in front of the pulpit, and the pews are of similarly high quality. The building now serves as a United Reformed Church. Seen from a distance the unusual tower still pierces Sunderland's skyline, making St George's one of the most prominent buildings in the city.

In 1892 the Presbyterians of North Bridge Street built the Free Church of Scotland to replace their former place of worship, the Scotch Church, a severe classical building by John Dobson (1827). The present church was designed by another Newcastle architect, William Lister Newcombe (1848–1929), and dedicated to the Revd John Black[166] [Fig 63]. Now known as Hebron Church, the building is a conventional Gothic Revival church with a tall nave and prominent spire. It was designed in the Decorated style, and the materials are rock-faced sandstone embellished with shafts of red granite. The main feature is the tall tower and spire, richly designed with corner buttresses that rise to a belfry stage with paired lancet openings. From the belfry rises a broach spire with bands of blind rustication, and strident gargoyles project from lucernes. The west face of the church has twin windows with an elliptical light between and the apex of the gable is pierced by lancets. The interior is divided by arches on fat piers of Shap stone. The pulpit and choir are raised on a platform and the sanctuary is panelled in wood with a frieze of Tudor flowers. Many of the windows have clear glass, but the large east window has stained glass depicting Christ and the Evangelists amid geometric patterns. The window in the east end of the north aisle was made by Atkinson Brothers of Newcastle (1892).

63 Free Church of Scotland, North Bridge Street, by W.L. Newcombe, 1892.

Fawcett Street Wesleyan Chapel was also sold for commercial development, as Fawcett Street ceased to be a residential area. Its successor, ★Durham Road Wesleyan Methodist Chapel, was opened in 1902. The design was open to competition and the winner was J. Jameson Green (1872–1945), who had been trained in Liverpool by C.O. Ellison, an architect favoured by Wesleyans. It was a large Gothic chapel with a spire and unusual tracery in the main window. The building was eventually demolished for road improvements.[167] Green's success led to him also building a ★Wesleyan Hall in Trimdon Street in a mixed style in 1902[168] and Ewesley Road Wesleyan Chapel in 1904. The latter used bright red brick and a free Gothic style, which was becoming fashionable at the turn of the century.[169]

Two other projects are worthy of note. The founders of the Salvation Army, William and Catherine Booth, had heard the American Holiness preacher Phoebe Palmer speak in Sans Street Wesleyan Chapel in 1859, and this inspired Catherine to take up preaching herself. The Salvation Army subsequently expanded its mission in Sunderland. A vast barracks was built on Roker Avenue and opened by General Booth in September 1883. This is credited to George Hildrey (1859–1933), even though he was a contractor rather than an architect. The Salvation Army built a citadel on the site of the Lambton Street Theatre in 1891. The national architect to the Salvation Army, W. Gilbee

Scott of London (1857–1930), provided a suitably warlike structure in bright
red brick and terracotta.[170] The building presented a bold castellated frontage
fortified with strong buttresses and battlements. A central block projected like
a gatehouse, flanked by side wings. Romanesque influence was evident in the
paired doors set within a vaulting round arch, which was filled with terracotta
tiles. An arcade of round arches ran above the entrance and the building
terminated with castellated parapets supported on arched corbels. The square
turrets were pierced by arrow-slits in the form of crosses. The date 1891 was
displayed on a painted ashlar panel in well-cut figures and a Lombard frieze
stretched between the turrets. The interior had a stage and gallery, along with
nineteenth-century detail in stucco. Resembling a medieval castle, the citadel
was a base from which the Salvation Army waged its war on sin.

In the new century came the first building that recognised Arts and Crafts
ideas when Cackett and Burns Dick of Newcastle won a competition and
built the initial stage of Roker Presbyterian Chapel in Side Cliffe Road (1910).
The entire design was never completed.[171] One Methodist church stands out
as not only one of the best buildings in the town but also as one of the most
important Nonconformist churches in the country. This is St John's Wesleyan
Church in Ashbrooke Road, which opened in 1888 [Plate 7]. Although
the membership at this time was small they were wealthy enough to make
St John's the most expensive church ever built in the town – at £17,000 it
was nearly double the cost of Prior's church of St Andrew at Roker some
twenty years later. St John's stands like a cathedral amid the leafy avenues of
Ashbrooke, dominated by a tall, piercing spire. In an era when most Methodist
places of worship were still classed as chapels, St John's status as a church was
unmistakable. The fabric is infinitely richer than any Methodist chapel then
erected in Sunderland, and its arrangement seems a model of Anglican liturgical
planning. Only the west-east orientation, in reverse of traditional Anglican
practice, hints that the building springs from a different denomination.

The stonework is rock-faced, but the courses are so neat and intricate that
the building has a rich, finely worked texture. From the soaring frontage
a gabled entrance porch thrusts forward and twin doors are enclosed
within a single arch – a device commonly used in cathedrals. The porch is
ornamented with swirling bosses and its apex overlaps with the vast five-
light window with wheel tracery above. Side aisles and a tall clerestory
run down the nave until the chancel juts out at the rear, thus fulfilling the
liturgical requirement that the sacred domain of the altar be expressed as a
separate volume. An unusual double transept emerges at the west end and
a low entrance porch obtrudes at the east. The dominant features are the
tower and spire, which were planned to be taller than those of neighbouring
Christ Church. Beginning from a massive base, the tower is subtly tapered,
the buttresses receding into the body before an octagonal spire refines it to a
single point. A spiral stair turret clings to the north transept and provides the

only means of access to the north gallery, which was reserved for the servants of the church's most affluent parishioners. The stairs were lined with lead in order to reduce the sound of their footsteps as they left services early to prepare coaches for their employers. Rich sculpture wells up between the lancet windows, and every gable ends with a foliated cross. Even the wrought-iron door-hinges are orchestrated into sinuous patterns, expressing the beauty of nature. Nestled between the gables of the north transept is a canopied niche that once contained a statue of the church's patron, St John. In many respects this is a church that resembles Anglican models. However, the extensive provision of ancillary rooms such as vestries, lecture hall, band room and schoolrooms demonstrates its Methodist traditions, even though their design alludes to medieval monastic planning.

Internally, the nave has pointed arches springing from slender round piers. The presence of side aisles precludes the sweeping galleries found in many Methodist chapels. Instead, the Methodist tradition has been adapted to fit the Anglican format and galleries are installed at the east end and in the transepts. The roof is of timber and its structural members come to rest upon elegant corbels. The chief benefactors of the church, Thomas Coke Squance (1828–97) and John Wallace Taylor (1834–1927), are commemorated in great windows that face each other along the nave. Squance was an accountant and keen antiquarian; Taylor was a ship owner, town councillor and member of the River Wear Commission. In the chancel, the Squance window features conventional stained glass, but its counterpart above the entrance is much more vibrant. A high chancel arch separates the chancel from the nave and a fully formed choir is housed beneath. Nearby, the pulpit is both decorous and richly symbolic. A line of scripture, 'Blessed are those who hear the word of God and keep it', encircles the base, and a handrail in the form of a serpent adds potency to this message.

The astronomical cost of the building was met by the wealthy residents of Ashbrooke, who were beginning to transform the character of Methodism in Sunderland from a traditionally working-class faith to something that matched their own higher status. This permitted the extensive use of ornament throughout the church. The building was designed by Robert Curwen (1849–1915), who had an extensive nationwide practice for Wesleyans. Curwen had been trained in Liverpool by C.O. Ellison before moving to London. He was the winner of the limited competition for The Leys School in Cambridge, which was built by the Wesleyans, so he must have been well known in Wesleyan circles when he gained the Sunderland commission, even though his career is now largely overlooked. In this church he produced one of the best examples of the use of Gothic architecture in a Nonconformist setting.[172] In 1887 the *Sunderland Daily Echo* described it as 'one of the most elaborate and inspiring places of worship in the town'.[173]

4

Commercial Buildings

As the population of Sunderland grew there was a need for more shops, business premises, hotels, public houses, theatres and leisure facilities to satisfy the demands of the inhabitants. Providing such services for the townsfolk gave businessmen many opportunities to make a profit. This process can be best examined by looking at the development of a Central Business District, which spread from its original location running parallel with the river on High Street East and West into Fawcett Street, Union Street and Holmeside, drawing the centre of the town southwards towards the main respectable residential district of Ashbrooke.

Shops and Banks

Traditionally, markets were the main facility for buying goods, and in 1830 *new markets for provisions were opened under the aegis of the Improvement Commissioners. It is possible that they were designed by Richard Dowell, the town surveyor, as he laid the foundation stone in 1829. In 1834 the *Royal Arcade was opened to provide an ornamental entrance to the market.[174] In 1880 *markets designed by J. and T. Tillman were built in Union Street to supplement the existing ones and to bring a facility closer to the new retail centre of the town. This was a private speculation and combined nineteen shops on the street and twelve open stalls within.[175] While these markets remained important and are still remembered, the growing trend was to build shops specifically designed for retail trades. The first important development was Hutchinson's Buildings in 1850–51 [Fig 64]. Occupying one of Sunderland's most prominent corner sites, these form a sober classical edifice at the intersection of High Street and Bridge Street.[176] This junction is known as Mackie's Corner, after a silk hat manufacturer who occupied the building for many years. The two grand elevations are pivoted around an indomitable corner drum that is domed and augmented with clock-faces and scallop shells. Giant pilasters scale the upper storeys, and the drum is surrounded by a circular colonnade of Corinthian columns. A bold

64 Hutchinson's Buildings by G.A. Middlemiss, 1850–51. This bold Neoclassical
building came to be known as Mackie's Corner.

entablature sweeps around the drum and a severe attic storey rises above.
The ground floor was constructed from cast-iron posts and stanchions, but
these are now obscured by plate glass. The ground floor was devoted to
shops and residential space was provided in the upper storeys. Hutchinson's
Buildings were built of high-quality stone obtained from Craigleath quarry
near Edinburgh, which had been praised by the committee researching
materials for the New Palace of Westminster (begun in 1834).

Hutchinson's Buildings were erected by the timber merchant and
shipbuilder Ralph Hutchinson. One of the earliest examples of full-blooded
classicism in Sunderland, the building was the focal point of the town's
burgeoning commercial district and a statement of prosperity that consciously
echoed the tradition of Tyneside Classicism. In particular, the bowed corner
is reminiscent of Newcastle's Central Exchange (1837–38). Unfortunately this
message is somewhat garbled. The architect, G.A. Middlemiss, was a semi-
professional figure who combined his architectural practice with an auction
business, and although the building is designed within a classical idiom it shows
a disregard for the strict principles of classicism. The discipline of the façade
collapses on the High Street elevation, with pilasters occurring at irregular
intervals. These problems were compounded when the building was damaged
by fire in 1898. Joseph Potts and Son rebuilt Nos 105–9 High Street in 1898–99
to the original design, but with a change in level that damages the unity of

the façade. It was also said that the internal arrangement of the building was inconvenient. The biggest problem was that while Newcastle had the visionary Richard Grainger to see through the extensive rebuilding of the town centre to an overall design plan, Hutchinson's Buildings remained a solitary example in Sunderland.[177] Nevertheless, the building was much admired when it was completed, with the *Sunderland Herald* publishing an illustration of it on 25 January 1850[178] [Fig 65]. In an act of self-promotion that seems to have been characteristic, Middlemiss had his name inscribed on the entablature.

Middlemiss was a powerful figure in Victorian Sunderland. He owned a brickworks, which made him independently wealthy, and he also served as a Tory councillor, which gave him political influence. He was born on 1 March 1815 in the Thornhill area of Bishopwearmouth to a father who migrated from farm work in Scotland. He had no formal architectural training, but started as 'a lowly toiler' with the building firm of J.C. Tone and went on to establish his own building firm by 1844.[179] By 1847 he was describing himself as an architect, surveyor, appraiser and auctioneer. His reputation was made by Hutchinson's Buildings, but he also owned the Cornhill Brickworks in Southwick, which gave him another vested interest in the growth of the town.

The next attempt to build in Fawcett Street to an overall design was the scheme for Woods' Bank in 1875–78. Unfortunately, the scheme was only a partial success. The Newcastle banking firm of Woods and Co. owned a large area of land, which at the time was occupied by the Fawcett Street Shrubbery. With considerable vision the firm projected a vast complex of buildings that would extend from St Thomas Street to Athenaeum Street, giving Sunderland a commercial district to challenge the might of Newcastle.

65 An early image of Hutchinson's Building. (Image courtesy of Sunderland Museum)

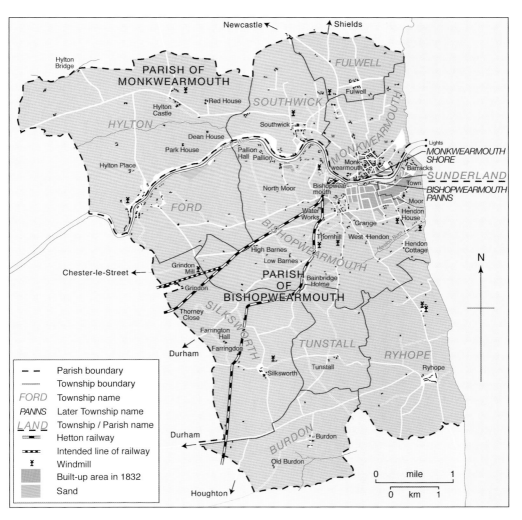

1 The three parishes of Monkwearmouth, Bishopwearmouth and Sunderland in 1832, together with their constituent townships. (By permission of the VCH Executive Editor. Copyright University of London: Cath D'Alton)

2 Holy Trinity Church was probably designed by William Etty in 1719.

3 St Ignatius'
Church, Hendon,
by C. Hodgson
Fowler, 1889.

4 The interior of
St Columba's Church,
Southwick, features a
mosaic floor and murals
by James Eadie Reid.
(Image courtesy of
Shaun Thubron)

5 The chancel mural at
St Andrew's Church, Roker.

6 St Andrew's Church, Roker, by E.S. Prior, 1904–07.

7 St John's Church, Ashbrooke, by Robert Curwen, 1888.

8 Elephant
Tea Rooms by
Frank Caws,
1873–77.

9 Gas
Company
Office, Fawcett
Street, by G.G.
Hoskins, 1867.

10 Dun Cow, High Street West, by B.F. Simpson, 1901.

11 The interior of the Mountain Daisy features a bar lined with faïence tiles.

12 Boardroom of the River Wear Commissioners Building.

13 Monkwearmouth station by Thomas Moore, 1848.

14 Langham Tower by William Milburn, 1886–91.

66 Austin, Johnson and Hicks's intended scheme for Fawcett Street, 1875–78.
(Image courtesy of Sunderland Museum)

The prime position in the centre was to be reserved for a new Subscription
Library and Literary Institute, while space in the adjoining wings and
pavilions was to be sold off commercially. Accordingly Woods and Co.
contracted the well-known Newcastle firm of Austin, Johnson and Hicks
to supply the designs, which effectively meant R.J. Johnson [Fig 66].
The architects envisaged a long parade of uniform classicism, dominated
by a projecting central block with a columned frontage. Matching north
and south pavilions would have stood at either end of the grand façade.
The enterprise was greeted with approval from the *Sunderland Times*,
which stated that 'public buildings in our town may almost be said to be
conspicuous by their absence'.[180] Unfortunately, local businesses were not so
enthusiastic; many of the buyers rejected the designs and hired their own
architects, though the Subscription Library did occupy the site next to the
bank with a glazed dome over the library hall. The southern wing was never
built and the library itself has since been obscured by a blank modern façade.
As a result, the building is only a glimpse of what could have been achieved.

Although the grand classical ambitions were severely curtailed, the actual
building is still a worthy addition to Fawcett Street and demonstrates Johnson's
expert use of classical forms[181] [Fig 67]. Woods' Bank occupied the north
pavilion, which successfully projects an image of impregnability. A sturdy
rusticated base supports the strong columns and opulent entablature. Banks of
this era sought to inspire confidence in their stability and this is no exception,
but a Baroque flourish emerges from within the sober classical lines. The arches
of the rusticated base are decorous and their keystones are elaborately scrolled.
A colonnade of giant Corinthian columns rises above, unfluted and pressed

67 Wood's Bank by Austin, Johnson and Hicks, 1875–78.

back against the façade, allowing the long stately windows of the *piano nobile* to come to the fore. Decorative cast-iron railings adorn each window and a Greek key motif runs beneath. The entablature is heavily ornamented and swells out to form a pulvinated (or cushioned) frieze. Prominent dormers are reared above the entablature with segmental and circular pediments alternating. As is typical in Fawcett Street, much of the ground-floor rustication has unfortunately been cut away and replaced with bland modern plate glass.

The siting of Woods' Bank led to a concentration of banks on that crossroads, though this was not uniformly the case. The dominant banking house in the town was that of the Quaker Backhouse family, based in Darlington, and in 1868 G.G. Hoskins built a new ★Bank on High Street, between the junctions with Norfolk Street and West Sunniside [Fig 68]. The renowned architect Alfred Waterhouse, who was also a Quaker, had designed their headquarters on High Row, Darlington, in the Gothic style. The bank adapted this style for all their branches in the region and Hoskins, who had been Waterhouse's clerk of works, became the architect who undertook this work.[182] Executed in Penshaw stone with dressings of Dunhouse stone, the building was crowned with three gables; each featured a panel bearing the arms of the Backhouse family. Like Hoskins's Gas Company offices (1867), the building had a Gothic oriel window in the centre, supported on a muscular column of red Aberdeen granite. The bristling façade was arrayed with balconies, some supported on consoles with grotesques carved to Hoskins's design. The crushing masses of masonry were typical of the High Victorian Gothic tradition. Inside, the banking hall was divided by an arcade on massive columns of red granite [Fig 69]. The floor was lined with encaustic tiles by Maw and Co.; the woodwork was of oak and Spanish mahogany. At the east and west ends were fireplaces of black marble relieved with Egyptian green and serpentine marbles. Hoskins designed furniture for the private offices, and the upper floors provided accommodation for clerks.[183]

68 Backhouse Bank, High Street, by G.G. Hoskins, 1868. (Image published in *Building News*, 3 March 1871)

The other major bank that was away from Fawcett Street was the National Provincial (1876) on the north-west corner of High Street and John Street [Fig 70]. This was designed by John Gibson (1817–92) of London, who was the bank's standing architect. Gibson had formerly worked as an assistant to Sir Charles

69 The interior of Backhouse Bank. The space was punctuated by massive granite columns and the floor was lined with encaustic tiles. (Image published in *Building News*, 10 February 1871)

70 National Provincial Bank by John Gibson, 1876.

Barry (1795–1860), which gave him a thorough knowledge of classical and
Renaissance styles. He was a highly accomplished architect who went on to
win the RIBA Gold Medal in 1890, and he designed over 120 bank buildings
between 1862 and 1881.[184] The National Provincial Bank established the
first truly nationwide branch network in Britain, and Gibson designed over
forty branches for the firm, including six in the North East: these represent
the single greatest geographical concentration of his work for the firm.[185]
The Sunderland branch is a refined and delicate classical design with extensive
decoration. All three storeys have rusticated stonework, giving a sense of
impregnability. The ground floor is punctuated by round-headed arches
with keystones. Ionic columns of exceptionally fine workmanship articulate
the upper storeys, between shell-shaped arches with rich ornamentation.
Crowning the building is a fine entablature with jewelled brackets and
dentilled cornice [Fig 71]. The classical façade masks a complex internal
division of public and private space. A banking hall occupied the ground
floor and the upper storeys housed offices and residential quarters for a
caretaker. The bank was the most expensive of Gibson's North East branches,
and Sunderland is fortunate to possess such a fine example of his work.

    As Fawcett Street continued to develop as the town's commercial centre,
Lambton and Co. of Newcastle built their Sunderland branch to the north of
Wood's Bank in 1889–91. A free treatment of the Italian style, the building

was designed by Charles R. Gribble (1834–95) of London. Gribble had succeeded John Gibson as architect for the National Provincial Bank, and was therefore experienced in the field of bank design. Lambton's was designed as a modern Renaissance palazzo. Mercantile dynasties of the Renaissance had erected town houses or palazzi, which served as both residences and places of business. Banks and office buildings of the Victorian period emulated this model: not only did the allusion to mercantile families such as the Medici convey immense prestige, but the model was ideally suited to the complex division of public and private space required by these institutions. Sir Charles Barry was particularly adept at the Italian Renaissance style and used it for numerous banks and clubhouses, including the Reform Club in Pall Mall (1837–41). In the palazzo model, the storeys are treated as separate compositional elements distinguished by their windows, and the façade is rarely divided by columns or pilasters.

Lambton's Bank stands on a plinth of grey granite, which is sculpted into balustrades along the Fawcett Street elevation [Fig 72]. Three tall storeys rise above the plinth and the building terminates with an attic. The ground floor is encased in rusticated stonework and Tuscan porches project from the outer bays. Cast-iron gates were provided for extra security. Bank architecture of this period had to achieve a delicate balance, conveying prosperity without appearing frivolous. Lambton's Bank is a sober design enlivened with hints of

71 Rich ornamentation to the arches of the National Provincial Bank.

72 Lambton's Bank by Charles R. Gribble, 1889–91.

opulence. The ground floor is enriched with round-headed windows divided by slender columns of red granite and the heads of Roman gods emerge from the pediments. An entablature supports the recessed windows of the first floor. These are framed with Ionic pilasters and dentilled pediments. In true palazzo style the building is crowned by an Italian *cornicione*, or massive projecting cornice. A Mansard roof rises above, augmented with dormer windows with scrolled pediments. The ground floor housed a banking hall, while the richer floors above housed private offices. Those on the first floor were occupied by the River Wear Commissioners until this important institution erected purpose-built premises in 1907.[186] The Italian Renaissance style would have seemed rather old-fashioned by 1890, but Lambton's Bank used the style to good effect and remains one of the most elegant buildings on Fawcett Street.

Across the road, the York City and County Bank had their house architect, Walter H. Brierley (1862–1926) of York, design a new branch in 1902–05.[187] The building has three storeys, the lowest of which is executed in a sparkling grey granite [Fig 73]. This gives the building the requisite strength at a time when banks used architecture to inspire confidence in their stability. However, the upper floors are faced with golden sandstone and the contrast between the materials is rather jarring. The stonework of the ground floor is rusticated, but the horizontal bands are pulvinated or cushion-like; it is curious to see such a hard stone treated in this way. The upper storeys are linked by Corinthian columns, and an entablature with modillioned cornice completes the design. The corner is canted, producing a narrow bay that houses the entrance. A box-like oriel window projects above the door, supported by strong brackets. Balustraded balconies and architraves provide further notes of richness. Other banks were built in the town, but these were subsidiary branches and were of less architectural significance.

The extension of the railway south of the river gave new impetus to the development of Fawcett Street as a commercial centre. Indeed, the demolition of some properties to construct the line and the subsequent compensation received by the business owners encouraged a burst of building. The man at the heart of this was Sunderland's own 'rogue-architect' Frank Caws, who came to dominate shop-building in the town. His most distinctive building is the Elephant Tea Rooms, built for Ronald Grimshaw in 1873–77, which strikes a discordant note within Fawcett Street both in terms of style and colour [Plate 8]. Grimshaw was a grocer who established a small empire of retail outlets in the town. The building looks like the fantastical collision of an Italian Gothic palazzo and a Hindu temple, executed in a combination of red brick, faïence and terracotta – producing a visually abrasive polychromy that accentuates the spirit of eccentricity in which the building was conceived. The three storeys are treated as separate compositional elements: horizontal strata that wrap around the elevations. The windows are strung

73 York City and County Bank by Walter H. Brierley, 1902–05.

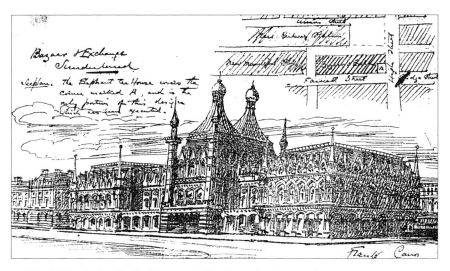

74 Frank Caws's sketch of a Bazaar and Exchange for Fawcett Street.
(Image reproduced from Caws's sketchbook)

together into miniature Venetian arcades, tinged with colour and divided
by slender pillars with foliated capitals. Surging through the horizontal lines
is a corner turret with a pagoda-like spire corbelled out from the bristling
wall surface. The turret evokes the form of an eastern minaret but abounds
in Gothic detail, including a coronet of gargoyles that radiate from beneath
a cluster of minute finials. The design reaches greater heights of fantasy in
the upper portions, where the roofline is broken into a series of sharp gables
punctuated by chimneys. Nestled between them are Gothic niches with
Indian elephants rearing their trunks beneath ogee arches. Caws described
the style as 'Hindoo-Gothic', and the elephants hint at the underlying
logic for such a bizarre hybrid of styles: they carry tea chests on their backs,
indicating that the building was an emporium for beverages and spices from
the Orient. Originally, the corner turret rested on a fan vault of terracotta.
Segmental arches adorned the lower reaches, with Gothic pillars mediating
between them. However, the windows were criticised for being too small
and failing to illuminate the interior sufficiently, and the ground-floor
ornamentation was swept away in the twentieth century.

The design was in part derived from John Ruskin (1819–1900), who had
championed the Gothic palazzi of northern Italy, with their spirited use of
polychromy, in *The Stones of Venice* (1851–53). Designs based on such palazzi
were common in Victorian towns, but Caws is unusual in combining them with
eastern styles. The fusion of Gothic and eastern styles was frequently attempted in
British Imperial architecture, but to import this into Britain, and especially into
Sunderland, is a forcible expression of Caws's eccentricity and exuberance. In his
sketchbook, Caws devised a fantastical scheme to develop the street in the same
style as the Elephant Tea Rooms by building an immense Bazaar and Exchange.

This would have extended from High Street to St Thomas Street; the present Elephant Tea House would have been repeated at every corner. The centrepiece was an ornate pavilion in an Islamic style, crowned with exotic pagoda domes and turrets resembling the minarets of a mosque. This was probably just a fanciful sketch, never likely to be built and possibly rather too much of a good thing, but the surviving element is a delight within the town, showing Victorian architecture at its most ornamental and eclectic[188] [Fig 74].

Caws designed several other shops in the next decade, and used these commissions to test his ideas about concrete floors to reduce the risk of fire. In this he showed his skills as an engineer, which supported his more adventurous design ideas.[189] This concern started when he was commissioned to replace the premises of Pearman and Corder, whose existing store had been burnt out in 1878. Opened in 1880, ★Phoenix House was a warehouse with a classical frontage to Union Street to act as the shop [Fig 75]. The ground floor was rusticated and pierced with segmental arches. The three central bays projected, as did the three outer bays at each end. Like the recently completed Sunderland Museum, the building revealed the influence of the French Renaissance style. Mansard roofs, dormers and *œil de bœuf* windows created a flamboyant roofscape and the building was named after the Phoenix carved above the central bay.[190] The warehouse was a monolithic structure built behind the classical frontage, but it was surmounted by a tower with a glass dome. The largest and grandest of Caws's new shops was ★Blackett's in High Street West, which opened in 1880 as one of the new department stores that were becoming fashionable. It was Italian in style and had two cupolas on the roof, but its ground floor had the latest plate glass windows to show off the goods[191] [Fig 76].

75 Phoenix House by Frank Caws, 1880. (Image courtesy of Sunderland Museum)

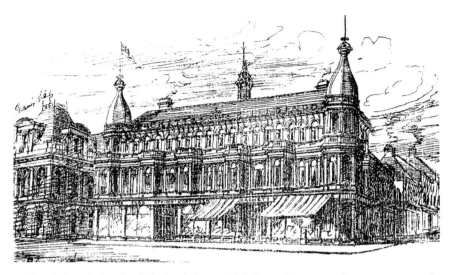

76 Frank Caws's sketch of Blackett's Store, High Street West, 1880. (Image courtesy of Sunderland Museum)

77 Sydenham House by Frank Caws, 1890.

Further up High Street, Caws built the ★Cobden Exchange in 1885, in a style described as Queen Anne by the newspaper. Despite Caws's best efforts the Exchange was subject to a fire in 1904, though it was probably the contents rather than the building that were to blame.[192] Finally, in 1890 he designed Nos 21–2 Fawcett Street for Corder's to replace their fire-damaged premises. The buildings rival the exuberance of Caws's own Elephant Tea Rooms. Corder House at No. 21 and Sydenham House at No. 22 represent an eccentric fusion of Gothic, Flemish and Baroque styles, and their vibrant colour is achieved by the use of red brick and masses of terracotta. Sydenham House is dominated by a projecting central section ending in a gable with a segmental pediment [Fig 77]. The gable has a wide-arched window with Gothic tracery. A griffin spreads its wings beneath the name of the building [Fig 78]. The first-floor windows are framed by granite pilasters and their heads are curvilinear in form, resembling contemporary Art Nouveau design. The ground floor has been replaced by bland modern shop-fronts, but a frieze with a miniature arcade still survives.

Corder House was built as premises for the draper Alexander Corder and is predominantly Gothic in style [Fig 79]. The ground floor has retained its fascia and frieze, supporting a balustraded balcony. The façade divides itself into two projecting bay windows that surge through the upper storeys to culminate in Flemish gables. The bay windows are so heavily ornamented that they resemble the plasticity of Baroque architecture. In another eclectic touch, the windows are framed by Gothic pilasters and foliage. A balustraded balcony

78 The gable of Sydenham House, with its fantastical griffin sculpture.

juts out at second-floor level, displaying shields with Gothic lettering, and the second-floor windows have an eccentric sinuous design. Above them, bay windows are recessed within elliptical arches. The twin gables are encrusted with terracotta ornament and pierced by oval lights, and a Gothic turret rises between them. The dates 1856 and 1890 are displayed on panels [Fig 80].

The contractors were David and John Rankin. The terracotta was supplied by J.C. Edwards of Ruabon in North Wales. Caws provided drawings for every brick and tile, which were then made in Edwards's factory and transported to Sunderland to be assembled on site.

79 Corder House by Frank Caws, 1890.

The fact that the pieces fitted together perfectly is a testament to the skill of both architect and factory. The fierce red appearance of the buildings and their eclectic mix of Gothic and Baroque styles again stand out in the street and were criticised at the time, but the buildings have now become treasured elements of the townscape and are best remembered as Meng's Restaurant. Despite his

80 The twin gables of Corder House.

eccentric designs, Frank Caws was a technically minded architect who was familiar with the latest building technologies. Both buildings have fireproof concrete flooring throughout, and wood and iron were used as sparingly as possible.[193] Caws kept his own office in Sydenham House, which suggests that he was particularly proud of the design.[194] He was active in professional circles within the North East, and in 1889 he was appointed the first president of the Sunderland Architectural Students association, where he taught classes on the engineering aspects of architecture.[195] Caws was also president of the Northern Architectural Association from 1901 to 1902.

Further shops were built in Fawcett Street, but curiously the best-known retailer did not do so. Binns, originally a draper's in High Street, had moved close to the new station at the southern end of the street in about 1885 to be nearer to the homes of their main clientele and to attract passing trade going to the station. Although they were not the first business in the area, they came to be a dominant firm. They adapted residential property and eventually spread through several houses, organising their store on American lines and extending their range of products. As a result, they only had alterations done while their rivals were building new stores. Binns only built proper department stores after the Second World War.[196]

Opposite Binns, ★John Coates the furnishers built a large store on the corner with Borough Road in 1882. The Tillmans designed a plain classical building with large windows, oriels on the first floor and a corner tower with a Mansard roof. This was acquired by Binns in 1903, but was destroyed by bombing in 1941.[197] In 1886 John Eltringham built ★Havelock House on the corner opposite Hutchinson's Buildings. This used new engineering techniques to eliminate the need for heavy supporting columns in the façade; instead, the building had load-bearing internal walls. Despite these technological innovations, the exterior was in a comforting French Renaissance style. It was completely destroyed in the major fire of 1898, which also damaged Nos 105–9 High Street on the opposite side of the road.[198]

An indication that new sites for shops were becoming needed was the building of Laidler-Robson in Holmeside in 1905. This four-storey furniture store and workshops replaced several smaller shops and was designed by Hedley and Greene in Queen Anne style. The building was executed in deep red brick with stone mouldings, but with steel stanchions to support the structure.[199] Another important element in the retail scene was the Sunderland Industrial and Equitable Society, which had been founded in 1858 and had premises in Green Street that had been extended over the years. In 1884 they decided to replace all the existing shops with a new ★Central Building to accommodate five shops around a three-storey central store and wings of two storeys. There were tailoring and shoemaking facilities at the rear, together with stables. A boardroom and lecture hall were situated on the first floor. The architectural competition attracted only

81 The former Co-operative Store on Southwick Green by W. and T.R. Milburn, 1897.

seven entrants and the winner was Robert Thompson Laidler (1837–97) from Holly Terrace. Laidler worked in Sunderland all of his life. In 1891 he registered as a clerk of works, which suggests that his architectural practice had failed. The building opened in 1887 and was subsequently extended.[200] The Co-op also built branches throughout the town, with Laidler designing one on Roker Avenue, at the corner with Church Street, in a similar style to Green Street (1889). The Milburns, who later became architects to the society, built a branch on Southwick Green in 1897, in red brick with flamboyant Dutch gables[201] [Fig 81].

The local historian James Watson Corder (1867–1953) notes that until 1870 Fawcett Street comprised respectable houses, but that commercial development then changed the character of the street, both by converting existing properties and by new building that was on a different scale. As it became the chief business street, he notes that it had 'few good buildings and many atrocities'. While Corder had a rather jaundiced view of newer developments and critical opinions of several local architects, his overall judgment seems fair, despite the attractiveness of some of the buildings: '[There was] no attempt to conform to any fine architectural scheme such as obtains in the best streets in Newcastle: the street from this point of view is an excellent example of a fine chance thrown away.'[202]

Industrial and Commercial Buildings

The buildings of Sunderland's expanding industries are not often to be found in the records. This may be because the architectural press declined to give such buildings much prominence and that, unless they were opened with some flourish, the local press did not cover the stories either. As a result there is little evidence of architects being involved with such projects. We know that Frank Caws designed workshops for Thompson's shipyard in 1894 and 1897 and developed a tank for testing models of ships' hulls, but apparently he undertook no larger projects for shipyards on the Wear. It may be that such work was done in-house by the company's own engineers. The same is true of Monkwearmouth Colliery, whose buildings do not seem to have been reported, and of Vaux Brewery. After the First World War the Milburns were architects to Vaux and carried out extensive and repeated additions to the brewery itself, as well as designing and altering many public houses.[203] Such factories that are recorded tend to be small, architecturally insignificant and more in the style of warehouses, where small-scale manufacture could be carried on. They have nearly all been demolished.

The greater size and complexity of Victorian businesses led to an increase in administrative personnel. This created a demand for office accommodation. Many small firms could manage with adaptations of existing houses, but larger organisations needed something more extensive, and several built dedicated offices. The Gas Company Offices at the end of Fawcett Street are a good example [Plate 9]. Needing a base where customers could pay their accounts, as well as offices for staff, the Gas Company chose a central site. The new office was a red brick edifice designed in the High Victorian Gothic style by G.G. Hoskins. It has two storeys plus an attic, with pointed dormer windows breaking from the roofscape. A powerful oriel window projects at the centre, resting upon a marble column with foliated carving. The muscular massing is typical of High Victorian Gothic, a phase of the Gothic Revival occurring in about 1850–70. Buildings of this period were strong and angular, and their robust forms were emphasised by the use of multicoloured building materials, a technique known as structural polychromy. The gas office is a prime example: red and blue bricks are combined with buff stone to produce a vibrant patterned surface. The building also reveals the influence of Venetian architecture. In the early 1850s art critic John Ruskin, who became enraptured by the Gothic architecture of Venice, published his previously mentioned monumental study *The Stones of Venice*, which inspired British architects to visit the city; and soon they began to incorporate Venetian motifs into their own work. In Hoskins's design, the horizontal division of the façade and the multicoloured windows echo Venetian forms.

High Victorian Gothic exemplified Britain's pride and confidence as the world's first industrial power. Using this bold and assertive style, the Gas Company announced its presence in Fawcett Street. This was the first commercial building in the street, and signalled its shift from an elegant, residential area to a bustling commercial thoroughfare. Despite there being no precedents for such an office building in that style, it makes an effective termination to the street, even though the ground floor is now a modern shopfront.[204]

Hoskins also designed furniture for the building, including chairs for the chairman and directors. These were executed in oak with ebony inlay in a Gothic style[205] [Fig 82]. The architect's brother, Walter Hamlet Hoskins (1845–1921), was a director and later vice-president of the North of England School Furnishing Company, and may have been involved in manufacturing the furniture.[206]

We have seen how other buildings in the central area – banks, clubs and shops – provided offices on the upper floors, which were let. Towards the end of the century full-scale office blocks were being speculatively built for rental. The firm of Henderson and Hall was active in the field of office design, building several dedicated offices for local companies. They built Sunniside Chambers for Botterill-Roche (1900–02) at the corner of Sunniside and St Thomas Street, as well as the Maritime Buildings (1900) on the opposite corner, for general letting. Both designs show the influence of Norman Shaw, particularly the corner turret reminiscent on a smaller scale of his designs for Scotland Yard.[207] The Maritime Buildings are constructed of red brick set off by horizontal bands of sandstone [Fig 83]. The design is in a free Baroque style, but like many commercial buildings of the period it reveals traces of Art Nouveau. The corner is canted and a slender turret springs from a

82 G.G. Hoskins designed Gothic style furniture for the chairman and directors of the Gas Company. (Image published in *Building News*, 17 September 1869)

83 Maritime Buildings by Henderson and Hall, 1900.

84 Sunniside Chambers by Henderson and Hall, 1900–02.

85 Central Buildings, West Sunniside, by John Hall, 1900–02.

wide ashlar bracket. The turret ends with a cupola of swirling drapery and an ogee roof with disc-and-spike finial. Shaped gables erupt from the roofline. The West Sunniside entrance has a panelled door set within a Gibbs surround – jutting blocks of stone pierced by Ionic columns – below an open pediment with dynamic keystones and rustication. Sunniside Chambers is similar to the Maritime Buildings, but is more muscular in form [Fig 84]. This three-storey office block is built of red brick with contrasting bands of golden sandstone. The upper floor is entirely lined with masonry, and concave panels recede into the wall surface between the windows. Rising at the corner, the turret tapers towards the summit and is crowned with an octagonal ogee roof.

John Hall of the firm of Henderson and Hall also designed the more conventional Central Buildings in West Sunniside (1900–02) [Fig 85]. Built as offices to let, the block has three storeys and a basement. One door has a entablature with pulvinated frieze and segmental pediment; the other has a swan-necked pediment and fluted pilasters. The windows are mainly plain sashes. A shaped gable crowns three bays at the right, containing paired windows between pilasters with a monogram in an aedicule. The offices came to be occupied by accountants and insurance brokers, but the basement was used as a snooker hall.

Hotels and Public Houses

The North Eastern Railway built hotels to serve their railway stations in many towns, such as York, Newcastle and Hull, but they did not do so in Sunderland. The ★North Eastern Hotel (1881) opened in Union Street near to the station, but this was designed by Joseph Potts and Son, and the NER would have used their own architects if it had been a company project.[208] The ★Queen's Hotel in Fawcett Street was already in business. Neither its date of building nor its architect is known, but it presented a long plain Georgian frontage to the street. The town centre had to wait until 1888 for a typically Victorian hotel to be built. This was the ★Grand Hotel in Bridge Street, designed by T.A. Page of South Shields. It was a four-storey design of three bays with differing pilasters on each floor and topped by fanciful dormers against the steeply pitched roof. A plainer extension was added to the north at a later date.[209]

As an industrial boomtown, Sunderland was bursting with commercial enterprises. One expression of this was the building of public houses with opulent interiors. These served as important recreational sites for the town's workforce. Many public houses and beerhouses in the east end were small and uninviting, converted from domestic properties. However, as breweries and other suppliers of alcohol became more powerful they sought to take control of public houses in order to have guaranteed outlets for their products. They were prepared to invest resources in creating establishments that were distinctive features in the townscape and provided various attractions to the

public. The design of these grander pubs became a specialist task, with much
effort being devoted to finding the most convenient way to service separate
bars with the minimum of staff. Many breweries appointed a standing architect
and therefore achieved something of a house style.[210] Among these specialists
were Joseph Oswald and Son of Newcastle, who were architects to Newcastle
Breweries. Joseph Oswald (1851–1930) was the son of the prolific Newcastle
architect Septimus Oswald (1823–94). He became a partner in his father's firm
in 1876 and assumed control of the practice when his father died in 1894. Oswald
was involved in the development of over a hundred pubs in the region, including
the Beehive Inn in Newcastle (1902). A particularly impressive example of his
work was the head office of Newcastle Breweries in Newcastle (1896–1901),
with its vibrant interior in turquoise and yellow faïence. The firm's work in
Sunderland included the rebuilding of the Wheatsheaf in 1898, the Foundry
Inn and the Blue Bell in Roker Avenue, both of 1901, and the rebuilding of
the General Havelock in Stoney Lane, Southwick (1904). The firm was well
known for its elaborate bar fittings, though most of these have been replaced.[211]

The Wheatsheaf public house formed one of Sunderland's most
prominent landmarks north of the Wear [Fig 86]. Its impressive design
is a rebuilding of a smaller pub that had occupied the site since 1828,
a simple three-storey building that stood at the junction of six roads.
Newcastle Breweries wanted to make better use of the prominent site
and commissioned Oswald to design a replacement. Built on a plinth of

86 Wheatsheaf public house by Joseph Oswald, 1898.

grey granite, the Wheatsheaf is a monumental Neoclassical edifice with a powerful curved façade. The ground floor is rusticated and two doorways are cut directly into the stonework beneath segmental pediments. In a favourite device of Oswald's, a Greek key motif runs above the windows. The upper storeys are articulated with Ionic pilasters, which have jutting blocks of rusticated masonry in their lower halves. A tall entablature completes the façade, with the name of the pub running around the frieze in bold letters. Wheatsheaf motifs are displayed on cartouches on the second floor. Surviving plans reveal that Oswald designed every detail of the interior himself, including elaborate wooden screens and stained glass. It was reportedly lit by a combination of gas and electric light. Some of the original fittings survive, but the woodwork was painted over in a recent refurbishment. Nevertheless, the Wheatsheaf survives as one of many opulent Victorian and Edwardian pubs designed by Oswald's firm.

The Newcastle architect Benjamin Ferdinand Simpson (1860–1940) had a distinctive style that he used for pub designs across the North East. In 1903 he built the *Grey Horse and remodelled the *Half Moon, both in High Street East. The Half Moon operated in an adapted private house, and Simpson was hired to transform this plain three-storey building into a more appealing venue. His solution was to aggrandise the façade without undertaking any substantial rebuilding [Fig 87]. The ground floor was clad in lavish stonework, culminating in an open segmental pediment that stretched the full width of the façade; the two original windows were encapsulated by a new oriel window with a spike finial.

Simpson's finest design in Sunderland is the Dun Cow in High Street West of 1901 [Plate 10]. This was a more substantial rebuilding of an existing pub. The owner Robert Deuchar employed Simpson to design an eye-catching corner pub that would lure in clientele with its sumptuous interiors of sparkling glass and lustrous wood.

The result is a splendid example of an Edwardian gin palace.[212] Simpson's four-storey building is a Baroque extravaganza that forms a fitting counterpart to the neighbouring Empire Theatre (1907). The building was constructed by the local contractor Thomas Pearson Shaftoe. Rising from a plinth of grey granite, the elevations have the animated plasticity typical of

87 Half Moon, High Street East, by B.F. Simpson, 1903. (Image courtesy of Sunderland Antiquarian Society)

the Edwardian Baroque style. Polished shafts of black marble rise from the plinth to support segmental hoods over the doors. Shallow bay windows project from the first floor, and the second-floor windows are linked by block rustication. The building terminates with intensely decorated Dutch gables, arrayed with scrolled forms and swan-neck pediments. A turret juts out from the corner, supported on richly carved brackets, and surges through the upper storeys to culminate in a copper dome. Simpson used similarly whimsical turrets in his designs for Emerson Chambers (1903) and the Manors Power Station (1903), both in Newcastle. Tall ashlar chimneys rise from the roofscape and the owner's initials, R.D., appear in the higher reaches of the building. Unlike many of Sunderland's historic pubs, the interior is remarkably well preserved, consisting of a main front room and a smaller sitting room at the rear. These are divided by an undulating wooden screen with panels of stained and frosted glass – its serpentine form an echo of the Art Nouveau style flourishing in Europe in this period.

Towards the end of the nineteenth century architecture began to emerge from stylistic revivalism. Architects and designers were turning their backs on the influence of the past and searching for new sources of imagery. Many turned to nature and to abstraction, developing a style based on swirling, sinuous lines. This was Art Nouveau, an exquisite decorative style named after Siegfried Bing's gallery *Maison de l'Art Nouveau* in Paris. The style was inspired by nature, but it was infused with a powerful sense of exoticism and the erotic. In the most extensive projects this style was used to create a mystical dreamworld in which the separate arts of architecture, furniture design and sculpture dissolved into one overpowering sensuous mass. Art Nouveau spread all over Europe, but had limited impact in Britain, where it was often deemed to be too risqué; however, many of Simpson's buildings flirt with this continental style. The most remarkable feature of the Dun Cow's interior is the decorative screen behind the bar, which fuses oriental and Gothic motifs into a screen resembling a theatrical stageset. Much of the woodwork has the swirling lines and whiplash curves of Art Nouveau. Inside the central arch is a cow's head, a playful reference to the pub's name. Overall the Dun Cow is an intoxicating fusion of Baroque and Art Nouveau devices, a heady concoction but one thoroughly appropriate for a rich turn-of-the-century pub.

Some of Sunderland's own architects designed pubs; for example, H.T.D. Hedley designed the Londonderry Arms (1901–02) for the Newcastle brewers Duncan and Daglish. This spectacular Edwardian pub occupies a triangular site on High Street West, which had previously been occupied by a pub called the Sign of the Peacock. The building was intended to be in keeping with the proposed court and fire station nearby, and for this reason it was designed in a relatively subdued Baroque style [Fig 88]. The irregular site was the result of a traffic management scheme and placed

88 Londonderry Arms by H.T.D. Hedley, 1901–02.

severe constraints on the architect. Hedley's solution was to make each façade unique. The north-west elevation has double doors at the centre, set within a rusticated round arch. An extremely delicate oriel window projects above the entrance. Dormers with triangular pediments break from the roofscape. The south elevation has a vehicle entrance cut into the façade. This potentially damaging feature is treated skilfully, set within a segmental arch matching those over the windows. The entrance is echoed by a portal in the first floor, framed by Doric columns. Triangular sites frequently cause problems for architects because they produce sharp corners, but Hedley solved this problem by placing round turrets at the north and west corners, capped with ogee domes and spike finials. However, the south east corner does not have a turret; instead, a porch is cut into the corner and the overhanging first floor is supported on a single column of granite. Some of the windows have etched glass displaying the name of the pub.

Hedley also designed the Tram Car Inn on Southwick Green in 1906. This is an exuberant small pub in Jacobean style with decorative tile work on the façade.[213] The narrow frontage is surmounted by an elaborate shaped gable, which ends with a ball and cushion finial. The ground floor is encased in lustrous yellow and brown faïence tiles. The three central bays have linked round arches with keystones on Corinthian columns. Cartouches and foliage occur between the arches, and a pulvinated frieze runs across the façade with 'Tram Car Inn' written in Art Nouveau letters. Beyond the richly coloured frontage, the sides are lined with white glazed bricks. Hedley was the tenth son of Thomas Fenwick Hedley (1821–94), a well-known estate agent in John Street. He was born on 5 April 1866 and educated in Sunderland and Harrogate. He trained with G.A. Middlemiss, then continued in partnership with Middlemiss's son in law under the style of Middlemiss, Green and Hedley from 1893. He was then in partnership with C.A. Clayton Greene from 1899 to 1905, before operating on his own. Acting as architect to both Thomas Turnbull of Fulwell and the Mowbray Estate meant that housing was the major element in his practice, although commercial premises such as the Tram Car Inn are his best-known designs.

W. and T.R. Milburn designed many pubs, but mainly after the First World War. In our period they designed the ★Bells Hotel in West Wear Street (1902–03) [Fig 89] and the Hat and Feathers, a remarkable small pub in Low Row (1903).[214] Now known as Green's, the building was designed for Charles Green and Co. The style is Baroque, but there are traces of exotic Art Nouveau in the details [Fig 90]. The pub is a symmetrical composition with three central bays beneath a steep triangular pediment. Short towers and ornate copper domes rise either side of the pediment. Within the pediment is a miniature window with rusticated pilasters, forming an aedicule. A wooden

89 Bells Hotel, West Wear Street, by W. and T.R. Milburn, 1902–03. (Image courtesy of Sunderland Museum)

90 Hat and Feathers pub, Low Row, by W. and T.R. Milburn, 1903. (Image courtesy of Sunderland Museum)

lantern rises from the junction of the roof ridges, terminating with a mace finial. The façade is lined with pink and grey granite, and the upper portions are executed in ashlar. Unusually, Green Man emblems appear between the Ionic scrolls. The Green Man was an ancient pagan symbol consisting of a grotesque face wreathed in foliage, and may have been included in reference to the owner's name. The words 'C. Green and Co.' appear above the doors in spirited Art Nouveau lettering. The Hat and Feathers was a well-composed building, but unfortunately it has not received all the care it deserves. The interior has been purged of its fittings, but originally it featured a U-shaped bar serving both select and public rooms.

The Milburns' most impressive work is the Mountain Daisy in Hylton Road (1901) [Fig 91]. A pub already existed on the site, but in 1900 the owner, W.B. Reid, hired the Milburns to design a spectacular drinking palace to compete with the new pubs being built throughout the town. The Mountain Daisy is a large red-brick pub fortified with sandstone dressings. The ground floor is lined with resilient black marble to protect the building from wear and tear. Designed in the Baroque style, it has a square corner tower enlivened with bands of sandstone. A series of shaped gables run along the roofline, and a metal plaque on the west elevation depicts – appropriately enough – a mountain daisy. Imposing as the exterior is, it is the interior that is truly impressive [Plate 11]. Originally there was a long front bar, with two smaller sitting rooms and a newsroom at the rear. In the

91 Mountain Daisy, Hylton Road, by W. and T.R. Milburn, 1901.

late nineteenth century a number of firms began to offer mass-produced decorative tiles, terracotta and faïence, sold through catalogues and used in many of the commercial and public buildings of the period. The buffet room of the Mountain Daisy has a quarter-circle bar glazed with yellow and green faïence. The walls too are lined from floor to ceiling with faïence, the hard, lustrous surfaces combining with a mosaic floor and rich woodwork to create an intoxicating effect. Although the tiles were mass-produced, some of them are painted as part of a unique decorative scheme. They depict historic sites of County Durham and Northumberland, including Bamburgh Castle, Cragside, Marsden Rock and the bridges of Sunderland and Newcastle. This work was executed by the firm of Craven, Dunnill and Co., based near Ironbridge in Shropshire. Founded in 1871, the firm was also responsible for the lavish interior decoration of Manchester Town Hall (1868–77). The Mountain Daisy boasted a wealth of wooden fixtures and stained glass depicting scenes of revelry. There was a large function room upstairs, retaining old bar fittings, a tiled fireplace and stained-glass windows.[215]

Places of Entertainment

In urban areas, as has been shown by the provision of parks, space for recreation had to be planned into the environment because traditional open spaces that could be used for leisure were eroded by development. This became more important as working hours were reduced, bank holidays and annual work holidays came in and weekly half-day holidays were made available to most of the working population. The provision of parks and other spaces of public recreation was designed to improve the health and physical fitness of the labouring population, and fresh air and exercise were prescribed as an antidote to the smoke and squalor of the city. Such facilities encouraged a healthy and therefore productive workforce. The development of the seafront was one response to these changes, as both commercial interests and the council provided facilities for visitors to the seaside. Equally, as sports became codified and more structured they needed specific locations where they could be played. Participant sports like cricket, rugby, hockey and lawn tennis were largely centred at the Ashbrooke Sports Ground, in a middle-class residential area and catering for people who could afford the subscription fees to join as playing or social members. It became a major regional venue for both rugby and cricket, hosting important matches in both sports. The ground was laid out in 1887 and the pavilion for the ground was designed in 1898–99, both by James Henderson (b.1861). The pavilion is a simple domestic-looking building, with large windows looking onto the cricket field.[216]

Association Football, despite its public school origins, had come to be seen as a more working-class game. Teachers, ministers of religion and others interested in youth work used it as a means of encouraging working-class boys to adhere to lifestyles acceptable to the middle class. Its popularity gave rise to professional teams playing in leagues and watched by increasing numbers of spectators. All this was facilitated by railways, which enabled teams to get to away matches, tramways, which enabled spectators to get to home matches on their Saturday half day, and the electric telegraph, which enabled the results of matches to be transmitted to local papers in time for a late edition to publish them. Sunderland AFC was formed out of the Sunderland and District Teachers Club in 1881. It joined the Football League in 1890 and needed a permanent ground that could accommodate the spectators who made it possible to attract and pay good-quality players. In 1898, after several moves, they finally settled on ★Roker Park, which was on the edge of a large working-class housing area and well served by the new electric trams. W. and T.R. Milburn planned a ground for 36,000 fans, which opened in 1899. There were facilities for players and club officials, but spectators had to stand on banking.[217] In 1913 it was decided to increase accommodation. A new and at the time novel terrace was built on reinforced concrete pillars to increase capacity to 55,000. This structure may have been designed by Archibald Leitch (1865–1939), who was the leading engineer of football grounds in the country. It was certainly Leitch who designed the grandstands in the 1920s and '30s to create the ★Roker Park that became famous throughout the Football League.[218]

The leisure activity that had the longest tradition of specifically designed buildings was the theatre. The ★Theatre Royal in Drury Lane was built in the 1760s by an unknown architect. In 1840 it was redesigned internally by William Beverley when the Beverley family took over as managers, and in 1871 it was extended and improved to become the New Wear Music Hall to designs by Thomas Moore and Sons, who were described as 'very experienced in this field'.[219] The reason the theatre became a music hall was that a new ★Theatre Royal had opened in Bedford Street on New Year's Eve 1855, designed by G.A. Middlemiss for the actor-manager Samuel Roxby [Fig 92]. This was an attractive, loosely classical design with a rusticated ground floor and a massive pediment, supported on two Ionic columns. The façade was heavily ornamented with a royal coat of arms and a bust of Shakespeare, both carved by James Hogg. William Beverley was again responsible for the interior design, and the building was hailed as an elegant addition to the street.[220] Given its location and the programme it presented, the theatre was intended to attract a middle-class audience. A rival to the theatre in Bedford Street was the Lyceum in Lambton Street, a coarse design in brick [Fig 93]. The three-bay façade was divided by giant pilasters and an oriel window emerged above the entrance. Opening with a performance by Charles Dickens's company in 1852, the Lyceum made a promising start,

92 Theatre Royal, Bedford Street, by G.A. Middlemiss, 1855. (Image courtesy of
Sunderland Museum)

93 Lyceum Theatre, Lambton Street, 1852. (Image courtesy of Sunderland Antiquarian
Society)

but it was dogged with bad luck. It was extensively altered internally in 1855 with Moore, William Crozier, Thomas Meik, J. Gillis Brown and James Lindley all credited with contributions to the architecture, engineering and decoration. Within months it had burned down, however, and had to be rebuilt by Moore with Joseph Potts. In September 1856 it saw the debut of Sir Henry Irving (1838–1905) on the professional stage. The second rebuilding of the Lyceum led the local historian William Fordyce to note that Potts became an eminent theatre architect. Certainly three other theatres were designed by the firm, and they are the only jobs that were completed outside the immediate area of Sunderland; Potts is not seen as a major figure in this field by the specialists in theatre history, however. In 1880 the Lyceum was destroyed by fire again and the ★Salvation Army built their citadel on the site.[221]

The audience for drama was never going to match that for the music hall, and as skilled workers increasingly had money to spend on entertainment, more halls were built to attract them. The ★Avenue Theatre on Gill Bridge Avenue was designed in 1882 by its builder Charles Dunn (1842–1926) with the help of Richard Thornton, the theatre manager. Edward Bell of London was responsible for the internal decoration. It had a distinctive stepped gable, which survived its incorporation into an expanded Vaux brewery in 1898.[222] In 1891 Thomas Angelo Moore built the ★People's Palace in High Street West, with restless classical decoration on the frontage [Fig 94]. It was described as the

94 People's Palace, High Street West, by Thomas Angelo Moore, 1891. (Image courtesy of Sunderland Museum)

first theatre specifically designed as a
'Theatre of Varieties'.[223] The ★Kings
Theatre in Crowtree Road opened
in 1906 to designs by William
Hope (1862–1907), an architect from
Newcastle who made an unexpected
reputation as a theatre architect with
some twenty-five commissions,
mainly within the region but
also elsewhere in the country.
The Sunderland design was one
of his last, and had a plain exterior
dominated by the six shops that
occupied the ground floor, though
with expenditure of £28,000 it was
intended as a palatial building.[224]

The one theatre that survives is
the Empire in High Street West
[Fig 95]. Among the grandest
of Sunderland's commercial
buildings, the Empire is a Baroque
palace overflowing with sculpture.

95 Empire Theatre by W. and T.R.
Milburn, 1907.

Making best use of the corner site, two asymmetrical wings are laid in
convergent streets; the angle between them is chamfered off and eclipsed
by a vast drum reaching high above the roofline. This cylindrical tower
is crowned with a dome of tarnished copper, where a cluster of slender
Ionic columns form a pedestal for a globe spun from thin strands of
metal. The figure of Terpsichore, the Greek muse of dance, stands at
the summit, brandishing a laurel leaf. The Empire features a wealth of
sculpture, as was typical of the Edwardian Baroque manner. The dome
is encircled by a balustered parapet with strident dormers breaking its
circumference. The tower is braced with vertical strips of masonry
adorned with lions' heads and festoons of flowers. Like many examples
of the period, the Empire actively avoids symmetry: the large, deeply
recessed window on the north wing contrasts with the Venetian window
of stained glass on the south. The theatre is entered through the base of
the tower, where a circular porch is framed by Ionic columns executed
in mahogany. Inside, the saloons and waiting rooms are decorated with
pilasters and fibrous plaster ceilings. The main staircase is composed of
terrazzo (marble chips embedded in cement) and lined with balusters of
wrought iron. The stairs rise in a grand curve to the palatial auditorium,
which comprises three sweeping tiers of seats with richly ornamented
balconies and a ceiling encrusted with plaster decoration. Beneath this

lavish surface, the cantilevered floors, roof and staircases are built of concrete in an attempt to make the building fireproof.[225] The theatricality of the Edwardian Baroque style made it ideal for the Empire, but it had a deeper resonance within contemporary architecture. Inspired by the work of architects such as Wren and Hawksmoor, this vigorous and unabashed style was felt to be a uniquely British variant of Baroque, and was frequently used to express the power of the British Empire during the Edwardian age, a period of great national pride. The Empire Theatre has been much altered and extended over the years, but remains one of Sunderland's best-loved buildings.

The architects chosen by Richard Thornton to design the Empire were W. and T.R. Milburn. The brothers had recently supervised a theatre in South Shields for Frank Matcham (1854–1920), the most famous theatre architect of the day. It proved an important commission because it gave them an introduction to the design of music halls. When Thornton moved on to manage the national Empire chain, he continued to use the Milburns to design and alter his theatres throughout the country, which was a valuable and high-profile connection. They handled thirty-seven projects up to the 1930s, and theirs was the only Sunderland architectural practice to have a reputation outside the North East. This was reinforced when both brothers served as elected members of the RIBA council. The biggest commission they won was the Dominion Theatre in Tottenham Court Road, London (1928–29). Specialists in the field do not rate their work highly, seeing it as professional but lacking in the flair and excitement essential for theatre design. Nevertheless, the Empire in Sunderland remains as a theatre liked by performers and treasured by the town.[226]

The life of some of these music halls was to be short, as the development of the cinema offered a new leisure facility at a cheaper cost to the audience and with the added element of technical novelty. Initially films were shown in temporary structures or converted premises. For example, the Monkwearmouth Picture House, which was the first permanent cinema in the town in 1906, was a conversion of St Stephen's Presbyterian Chapel at the end of Wearmouth Bridge. It was a success, and enabled the Black brothers to develop a profitable career running cinemas; it also provided an incentive for others to do likewise.[227] By the First World War several cinemas had been opened, with the Milburns designing most of them, such as the ★West End Electric Cinema in Silksworth Row (1912), the ★Theatre de Luxe Cinema in Fawcett Street (1912), the ★Queen's Hall Cinema in Bridge Street (1913) and the ★Millfield Picture House in Hylton Road (1913).[228] While all of these claimed to reflect the latest innovations in cinema design, they were all quite small and made little impact on the streetscape. The building of the ★Havelock Cinema on the corner of Fawcett Street and High Street, where Havelock House had stood before the fire, set new standards. This was to be a luxury cinema on a site costing £60,000, and the design included shops, offices and a café. The interior of the cinema accommodated 2000 customers and, along with the café, was in Louis XIV style. The architects were Browne and Glover from Newcastle, who were gaining a reputation as cinema specialists, and it was the first example in the town of a grand cinema that would attract custom from all social classes. It initially boasted a ten-piece orchestra to accompany the films.[229] The Blacks also commissioned specialists Gibson and Steinlet of Newcastle to build their prestige cinema in 1912, the ★Picture House in High Street.[230] After the war there was even greater cinema-building activity when national chains erected extravagant Art Deco buildings designed by their house architects.

5

Transport

The vast scale of Sunderland's industrial development necessitated a complex infrastructure and wide-ranging transport networks. Colliery railways were extended across the countryside, staithes grew up along the banks of the Wear and new docks and coal ports were established. Transport became a substantial industry in its own right and a large employer. As a thriving commercial centre, Sunderland also required transport networks to enable efficient transit of goods and people. Throughout the period under study the town was augmented with railways, bridges and a public tram system. The construction of these new networks involved considerable feats of engineering, producing structures of impressive scale and design. They also generated more 'architectural' structures, including railway stations, offices for administration and warehouses. The resultant transport infrastructure was vital for Sunderland's industrial, commercial and leisure interests.

River

As a port Sunderland can be seen as a transport town, and the development of the river and its facilities was central to the town's prosperity in the nineteenth century. Although Sir Hedworth Williamson built a dock on the north side of the river in 1831–38, it was the River Wear Commissioners who were the key players in the creation of the thriving port. The North Dock (1834–38), despite being designed by Isambard Kingdom Brunel (1806–59) and with a ★Dock Office by John Dobson, was not a success as it was too small.[231] Brunel's other plan in the 1830s for a suspension bridge across the river came to nothing.[232] It was John Murray (1804–92), who was appointed engineer to the River Wear Commissioners in 1832 at the age of only twenty-eight, who created the docks that transformed the river. Murray had made various improvements to the river and its access, including the famous transportation of the lighthouse along the extended North Pier in 1841, which won him the Telford Medal from the Institution of Civil Engineers.[233] In 1832 he proposed a cut through Monkwearmouth to convert a bend in the river into a dock, and in 1842 suggested lock gates across the river mouth to maintain a constant depth of water in the river. Both these ideas were rejected as being too radical. He then produced proposals for a dock controlled by lock gates on the south side of the river, and when George Hudson took up the idea he became engineer to Sunderland Dock Company (in 1845), while remaining consultant to the River Wear Commissioners. Initially the project involved Robert Stephenson, but when the Parliamentary Act was achieved in 1846 Stephenson withdrew, and Murray became wholly responsible for the design and construction of docks and a tidal basin with one access to the river and another directly to the sea to the south. The docks were opened in 1850, though additional works went on into the 1860s.[234]

In 1850 Murray designed an office for the Sunderland Dock Company [Fig 96]. Built of limestone with sandstone dressings, the office is a compact cube, two storeys tall and three bays wide. A projecting wing at the east houses a staircase, and a tower rises at the south-east corner. Unusually for its date and industrial purpose, the office was designed in a Baroque style, which is expressed in the blocky rustication throughout. The ground-floor windows have rusticated surrounds and plain lintels; the first-floor windows have architraves with voussoirs and long keystones, and quoins occur at the corners. The building is crowned with an entablature and a hipped roof surmounted by a chimney. The doors are panelled and set under architraves.

96 Office for the Sunderland Dock Company by John Murray, 1850. The Gladstone Swing Bridge is visible in the foreground.

Some original stucco decoration survives. A hydraulic accumulator was inserted in about 1875 for the nearby Gladstone Swing Bridge, designed by Sir W. Armstrong and Co. for the River Wear Commissioners.

As Murray took responsibility for the docks in 1845, Thomas Meik (1812–96) became engineer to the River Wear Commissioners, and when they bought the South Docks in 1859 he had charge of all the works in the port. He built the South Pier with its lighthouse in 1856. The lighthouse takes the form of a tapering Tuscan column surmounted by a gallery and dome [Fig 97]. A plaque above the doorway bore the image of a sextant and the date 1856. The interior has a cast-iron spiral staircase. It was superseded when the new piers were built between 1885 and 1907, and was moved to its present site at Roker Cliff Park in 1983 when the old South Pier was shortened. Meik also built Hendon Docks as an extension to the existing facilities in 1868, and a range of staithes and other facilities. Most of these were constructed by the River Wear Commissioners' labour force, including the Hendon Dock, which meant that Meik had a heavy load of supervision as well as design work. In 1868 he resigned to establish a consulting engineers practice with his sons, which still exists today as the Halcrow Group.[235] John Dobson designed a ★grain warehouse in the docks in 1856 and Meik added ★another in similar style in 1863. They followed the pattern of Jesse Hartley's dock buildings at Liverpool and were impressive in their simplicity. Each was a monolithic structure built of brick in the most severe Neoclassical style. Gaping round-headed arches ran through the first floor, below four floors expressed by plain square windows. Simple cornices and pilasters relieved the stark wall surfaces and both structures terminated with parallel hipped roofs. They were positioned on the western edge of the dock, facing out to sea. Dobson's block was the larger of the two; it had *œil de bœuf* windows in the ground floor and the fourth bay was double the width of the others. As Sunderland largely shipped coal, however, the main requirement was for staithes and coal drops, and these two warehouses remained isolated examples.[236] The banks of the Wear were once lined with

97 Thomas Meik's lighthouse was built on the South Pier in 1856, but was relocated to its present site at Roker Cliff Park in 1983.

immense coal staithes, most of which have been lost. However, the remnants of one such structure survive near the Stadium of Light. Built in about 1900, a brick-faced platform extends from the high ground at the level of the former Wearmouth Colliery, supported on three stages of brick piers [Fig 98]. Originally a wooden superstructure was built upon the platform and extended to a point high above the shore. This supported the railway line and sloping conveyor from which coal wagons could tip coal into the holds of waiting ships.

Henry Hay Wake (1844–1911) succeeded Meik in 1868, having been his pupil and assistant. He remodelled the docks and was in charge of the building of the long breakwaters, which

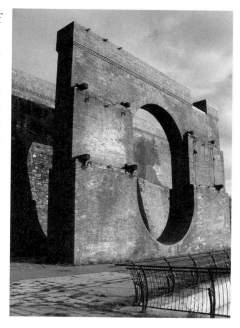

Surviving remnants of the coal staithes below the former Wearmouth Colliery. These were built in about 1900.

were begun in 1883. Two piers were planned by Wake, but only one was completed. The north pier is over 900yds in length and reaches out to sea in a bold quadrant curve. The pier was built with a rubble and cement foundation faced with blocks of concrete and red Aberdeen granite, making the overall structure red and white. A lighthouse was built on the pier head in 1903. The tower is composed of alternating red and white bands; the red bands are rock-faced, producing a variation in texture as well as colour. The lantern is surrounded with an iron gallery, with a second gallery running around the domed summit. Deeply recessed windows are cut into the tower. This lighthouse had what was in 1903 the most powerful port light in the country. The cast-iron railings along the pier are tapered and round, with lozenges at the centre, and lampposts of the same design are incorporated. Cottages for lighthouse keepers were built at the shore end. The foundation stone for the pier was laid on 14 September 1885 and construction was completed on 23 September 1903, as recorded on a dated stone. The south pier was partially constructed, but abandoned in 1907. The piers were therefore still unfinished at the time of Wake's death, but remain the most striking features of Sunderland as a port.[237]

The River Wear Commissioners built a swing-bridge south of the sea lock in about 1875, which gave access to Hudson Dock from the north. Known as the Gladstone Bridge, it was named after four times Prime Minister William

Ewart Gladstone (1809–98), who also opened the bridge. The hog-back structure was built of riveted steel girders. The east end is enclosed by a sweeping stone wall. When the bridge is closed the west end rests on a stone abutment. It was operated by engines and an accumulator housed in the adjacent dock office; the hydraulic machinery was manufactured by Sir W. Armstrong and Co. of Elswick and is an early example of the hydraulic technology developed by Armstrong. Wake also designed a swing-bridge of very similar design on the east side of the Hudson Dock in conjunction with a new lock and water channel that opened in 1880. This is an asymmetrical hog-back bridge constructed from steel girders. Vertical and diagonal struts are riveted to the superstructure. The bridge pivots on the north lock wall and was also operated by hydraulic machinery made by Armstrong and Co. The date 1880 is given on a plaque, which also records the contributions of Wake, the River Wear Commissioners and the contractors Andrew Handyside and Co. of Derby and London. Surviving near the bridge is a fascinating piece of industrial archaeology, a machinery pit for the lock gates. This was built in 1880 by Wake for the River Wear Commissioners, as recorded on a round cast-iron plate in the dock workshop. The interior of the pit is lined with ashlar, and an array of cast- and wrought-iron wheels, cogs and chains is still visible.

A new Customs House was built in about 1900 in West Sunniside to regulate activity in the port. Designed by an unknown architect, probably within the Office of Works, the building is thoroughly domestic in tone; a sharp gable crowns the principal bay at the right and a dormer window breaks from the roofscape [Fig 99]. A powerful Diocletian window dominates the ground floor, further emphasised by jutting blocks of rustication around its circumference. The door is set in a receding bay within an architrave of pink granite. Originally there was a carved and painted royal coat of arms above the door, which belied the building's domestic character and revealed its official role as a customs house. Tuscan pilasters frame the windows and scrolled brackets support the cornice. Extremely tall chimneys run parallel to the ridge of the gable. [238]

As well as all their work on the river, the River Wear Commissioners built an office building in John Street

99 Customs House, West Sunniside, *c.*1900.

with a grand meeting room for the Commissioners, though it took them a surprisingly long time to do so. The Commissioners had originally operated from the Exchange Building, then from offices above Lambton's Bank in Fawcett Street, but in 1904 they resolved to erect a purpose-built office in the town's business district. A site was selected on St Thomas Street and a design competition was held. This was won by the local firm of Henderson and Hall, who specialised in office design. John Hall (1869–1935) was born in South Shields, the son of a shipowner. He was educated at a college in South Shields and at architecture classes before being articled to J. and T. Tillman in Sunderland. He attained First Class in his Architecture Examinations and Honours in Building Construction, and began practice in 1895 in partnership with James Henderson; but Hall took over as sole practitioner when Henderson moved to Canada in 1906. He was active in the Northern Architectural Association and Sunderland Antiquarian Society, where he pursued his interests in architectural history and archaeology. He was chairman of the society in 1914–15 and designed its badge, which combined the Saxon door of St Peter's Church with the Cross of St Cuthbert. Hall was a particular authority on Celtic and Saxon crosses and published papers on these topics. He was also a Freemason and served as Master of the Fenwick Lodge. Less is known about James Henderson, except for his partnership with Hall and that he captained the cricket team at Ashbrooke (which explains why he designed the cricket ground).

John Hall was the partner in charge of the River Wear Commissioners project, and the building opened in 1907 [Fig 100]. Rising from a rock-faced plinth of red Scottish granite, the building is an elegant composition in a free Baroque style. At each corner the outer bays project under open segmental pediments with florid decoration. Banded rustication runs through the ground floor, but in the upper storeys the rich decoration is crisply executed in pristine, blue-tinged stone. The principal windows of the first floor have curved pediments and block-like rustication. The door is framed by jutting stone blocks pierced by columns. Another curved pediment forms a canopy and supports the delicate oriel window that rises above the entrance. The building was a monument to the River Wear Commissioners and the image of a sextant is emblazoned above the doorway amid decorative mouldings. By opening the town to international commerce, the Commissioners allowed a wide variety of goods to be imported, including building materials. Accordingly the building uses a range of building stone and exotic woods from around the world. The blue-tinged stone used for the main body was dug locally from Heworth Burn, but no fewer than five separate varieties of marble were employed in the vestibule, including Skyros, Verde Antico and Bleu Belge [Fig 101].

The building houses one of the best interiors in Sunderland, and all the interior fittings were designed by Hall. At the core of the building is

100 River Wear Commissioners Building, John Street, by John Hall, 1907.

101 The segmental pediment above the entrance contains a cartouche bearing the image of a sextant.

a central hall, surmounted by a coffered dome with a glazed oculus that turns the space into a vast well of light. An elegant staircase with slender balusters rises around three sides. From floor to ceiling the walls are lined with gleaming panels and pilasters of Austrian oak; additional light is provided by a large window of frosted glass. The floor is lined with black and white tiles that contrast with the dark lustre of the wood. Originally the River Wear Commissioners would have met in the board room, a large rectangular chamber bounded at either end by stately fireplaces [Plate 12]. Reflecting the room's high status, the fireplaces are carved from expensive Cuban mahogany and lime-wood in the style of Grinling Gibbons (1648–1721), a talented sculptor and woodcarver who worked at St Paul's Cathedral and Blenheim Palace. The pilasters are mantled with flowers and exotic fruits suspended from cherubs' heads. The shallow curve of the ornate plaster ceiling is adorned with garlanded ribs painted in delicate blue and gold. Again, the variety and quality of the stonework and the exotic woods emphasise that Sunderland was a gateway to the world economy as a result of the efforts of the River Wear Commissioners. As stated in the *Sunderland Year Book* of 1907, 'No expense was spared in order to make the building thoroughly worthy of the important body at whose instigation it was erected.'[239]

Railways

The development of the port was greatly facilitated by the growth of railways to bring coal from the neighbouring pits to the river. Initially the wagonways were built by the coal owners, but soon the railway companies took responsibility. They soon came to realise that passenger traffic as well as goods traffic could be profitable, and this meant that they needed to build stations. As George Hudson (1800–71) was the prime mover behind the docks, so he was behind the railways and came to be known as the 'Railway King'. It is to him that Sunderland owes the splendid station at Monkwearmouth (1848), which replaced very inadequate facilities that existed near the Wheatsheaf [Plate 13]. Hudson was an industrialist with political ambitions. His business enterprises allowed him to finance the building as part of his successful election campaign as MP for Sunderland in 1845. To design the station Hudson acquired the services of the town's most respected architect of the early Victorian period. Thomas Moore had designed a number of mansion houses for private clients, and his sophisticated grasp of contemporary tastes culminated in his design for the station, a supremely elegant building in the Greek Revival style. The building is symmetrical about an imposing portico, its sober triangular pediment borne on four Ionic columns. Joined to the centre are low wings, which recede from the road in quadrant curves. Each is articulated with tall rectangular windows and paired pilasters. An impression of strength is contributed by the rounded entablatures, which are supported on fluted Doric columns. Raised on an elevated site, the building achieves a sedate elegance that entirely belies its industrial purpose. Even the railway track is politely concealed behind a screen of round arches and pilasters. Monkwearmouth station is the finest classical building in Sunderland. Moreover, its authenticity and harmonious proportions make it one of the most elegant buildings of its kind in the country. The architectural historian Sir Nikolaus Pevsner admired the building: 'If one does not mind a railway station looking like a Literary and Scientific Institution or a provincial Athenaeum, then Monkwearmouth is one of the most handsome stations in existence.'[240]

Monkwearmouth station was the Sunderland terminus of the Brandling Junction, which linked the town with South Shields and Gateshead. It was built close to Wearmouth Bridge for the convenience of passengers, which along with the stately design indicates that the station was intended primarily for passenger rather than goods traffic. The building is now a museum that retains an early twentieth-century interior. The internal volumes make the original layout comprehensible. The central block housed the ticket office and accommodation for the stationmaster. A first-class waiting room with moulded plaster ceiling occupied the south wing. In the north wing, the second-class waiting room was smaller and less elaborate, reflecting its lower status. From the central block, sliding doors lead to the platform, which is roofed with a canopy of iron and glass manufactured by the local glass-maker James Hartley and Co.[241] Though it is undeniably the showpiece of the enterprising Railway King, the building is a testament to the taste and skill of its architect.

Indeed, Thomas Moore was considered the 'father of the architectural profession' in Sunderland, and for many years was seen as the only architect the town possessed.[242] This is not quite true, as James Hogg and William Drysdale were in practice at the same time, though it could be argued that they were more surveyors than architects. Moore was born in Pallion, the son of a blacksmith, and was baptised at St Michael's Church, Bishopwearmouth. He began his career as a joiner and builder, but by 1844 was listed in directories as an architect. Details of his architectural training are obscure, but with so little competition in the town he was able to gain several important commissions. His practice was a general one, though he became known as a designer of theatres in the North of England. Moore was more comfortable working in the classical idiom, as with the group of buildings around Monkwearmouth station and the large houses he built for local businessmen. The station was his best design, but for many years it was attributed to John Dobson because architectural historians assumed that a building of such quality must have been designed by the region's best-known architect. Moore worked in the Gothic style when required, as at St Andrew's Church, Deptford, and Bishopwearmouth Cemetery.

From 1833 until his retirement in about 1864 he acted as surveyor to the Commissioners of Wearmouth Bridge and was also engineer to the Hetton Coal Company and surveyor to the Bishopwearmouth Highways Board. He married a local girl, Susan Canny, and they had three sons and three daughters. Thomas Angelo Moore (1840–91) and John Hutchinson Moore (1841–77) entered their father's firm, which was then styled Thomas Moore and Sons. Thomas Angelo continued in practice, establishing a considerable reputation as a theatre architect, until his sudden death in 1891. In the 1860s they opened an office in Leeds, probably to oversee their work as architects to the York Circuit of Theatres. The Leeds office later became the centre of the firm's operations. Thomas Sr retired in favour of his sons in the 1860s, though he served as president of the Northern Architectural Association in 1867. He died of 'natural decay' on 24 August 1869.

The building of the station gave a focus to North Bridge Street, and Moore designed the ★Royal Hotel and a ★Savings Bank, both in the classical style, in the street in the 1850s. Although Hudson gave Sunderland its finest railway building, it was the North Eastern Railway Company that carried out most of the important schemes. Monkwearmouth station, for all its elegance, was not ideal for many inhabitants as it was on the wrong side of the toll bridge, which was a notorious traffic bottleneck. The scheme to bring the railway over the river and to build a new station was largely due to Thomas Elliot Harrison (1808–88), who was chief engineer to the NER and one of the most highly respected figures in the railway industry. He was born in Fulham on 4 April 1808, the son of an employee at Somerset House. His family moved to Fulwell Grange, Monkwearmouth, to start a shipyard on the Wear. Harrison completed his education at the Kepier Grammar School in Houghton and was apprenticed to W. and E. Chapman, engineers and surveyors in Newcastle, where he came into contact with George and Robert Stephenson.[243] Harrison lived at Whitburn for much of his adult life. His first major job in 1836–38 was to supervise the construction of the Victoria Bridge, hidden away on the Wear below Penshaw [Fig 102]. Designed by Burges and Walker of Aberdeen, it was a crucial link in the London to Edinburgh route until Durham Viaduct was built in 1872.[244] The bridge was based on the Roman viaduct built by the Emperor Trajan over the Tagus river at Alcántara in Spain. The rails passed 135ft above the river, carried on four colossal arches, as well as three smaller approach arches at either end. The middle two arches have spans of 160ft and 144ft, and the outer arches each have a span of 100ft. Indeed, the Victoria Bridge has the second longest single span of all surviving masonry railway viaducts in Britain, exceeded only by the Ballochmyle Viaduct in Ayrshire (1846–50).[245] It was officially opened on 28 June 1838, the day of Queen Victoria's coronation, but did not open to traffic until the following year. Seen from a distance, the bridge makes a striking counterpart to Penshaw Monument, which stands on the

102 The Victoria Bridge at Penshaw was designed by Burges and Walker and
constructed by Thomas Harrison, 1836–38.

103 Wearmouth Railway Bridge by Thomas Elliot Harrison, 1874–79.

hill nearby. As Pevsner memorably asked, 'Is there any other place where one can stand beneath a "Roman" viaduct and see a "Greek" temple?'

In 1874 Harrison proposed to extend the line from Monkwearmouth over a bridge and into Union Street by using a cut and cover process that would place the platforms of the new station underground – a decision that has caused problems for the station to this day. The Wearmouth Railway Bridge was constructed from wrought-iron box girders with two cross-braced ribs, and was approached from the north by a masonry viaduct [Fig 103]. The utilitarian design is segmental in form, with elliptical openings in the structure. The bridge has a span of 300ft and runs 86ft above the high-water mark, reportedly making it 'the largest Hog-Back iron girder bridge in the World'.[246] It was opened in 1879, finally linking the NER's lines north and south of the river. Harrison was president of the Institution of Civil Engineers from 1873 to 1875. He kept his office in Newcastle Central station, and he was working there when he died only a fortnight before his eightieth birthday.[247]

Harrison's bridge has become one of the enduring images of the town, but the *station (1879), which was designed by William Bell (1844–1919), NER architect for thirty-seven years, was not a success [Fig 104]. The station was a High Victorian Gothic building in polychrome brick and stone. Its original design was condemned as contemptible. The council wanted a completely new station on a different site, but the railway company refused to build it.

After protracted negotiations the railway company eventually agreed to spend £40,000 on upgrading the existing station.[248] Bell replaced the High Street entrance with a portico and clock-tower, but these were poorly proportioned and grossly detailed, contrasting poorly with his best station design, Bank Top station in Darlington (1884–87). The clock-tower was stolid in form, with corner turrets and spire, and sat astride the eight-bay frontage. At ground-floor level a vast portico spanned the entire frontage, large enough to allow carriages to drive up to the station doors. The engine shed to Athenaeum Street was purely functional and did little for the streetscape. It was built of brick with a roof constructed from elliptical iron ribs. Running

104 Central station by William Bell, 1879. (Image courtesy of Sunderland Antiquarian Society)

along the length of the roof was a
central ridge ventilator – a pitched
canopy of glass to illuminate the
concourse and allow smoke from
the engines to escape. Externally,
the broad arch of the roof enclosed
three openings resembling
Diocletian windows [Fig 105].
The whole scheme was completed
in 1879.[249] The station was
destroyed in an air raid in 1940.

105 A print showing the engine shed of Sunderland
station. (Image courtesy of Sunderland Museum)

Much additional work was
done by Bell in the town, including a vast set of *stables in Easington Street,
Monkwearmouth (1883–84). This structure was predominantly built of
red brick, but polychromy was achieved by the use of blue brick and ashlar
dressings. The main elevation had a two-storey central section flanked
by single-storey wings of eleven bays. The stable courtyard was entered
through a large segmental arch in the centre of the façade, below a dormer
with *œil de bœuf* window. The arch had cast-iron wheel buffers at the base
to protect it from traffic in and out of the stables. Inside the courtyard the
inner façade had a similar central archway and dormer. The inner courtyard
contained a horse hospital. A single-storey van shed was added at the south
in about 1912.

106 Burdon House was designed by William Bell, probably with the assistance of his
deputy Arthur Pollard, 1914–17.

Bell also designed the restrainedly classical offices and shops opposite the Museum in Burdon Road (1914–17), built during the First World War[250] [Fig 106]. Known as Burdon House, this building forms an impressive landmark on an important route into the city. The ground floor has rusticated stonework and pilasters. The entrance is set within the final bay, before the façade breaks into a sweeping curve around the corner. Framing the door is a composition of rusticated stone and a round-headed surround. Giant Ionic pilasters punctuate the upper storeys between pairs of sash windows. The first-floor windows are framed with architraves and those in the second floor with segmental architraves and keystones. The main entablature has a dentilled cornice and supports a balustraded parapet. The south elevation has twin oriel windows, tripartite in form. The entrance bay is emphasised with a projecting balcony and open pediment, within which is a large cartouche displaying the date 1916. Bell retired in 1914 after more than fifty years' service to the company. He was succeeded by his deputy Arthur Pollard, and it is possible that Pollard had more to do with the detailed design process. The offices in the upper storeys were probably used by the NER, and the shops below would have provided a rent to offset the cost of the building.

A final significant edifice was the Queen Alexandra Bridge, which was built to allow coal from Washington pits to be brought to the South Dock (1908–09) [Fig 107]. By an agreement with Sunderland Corporation, who wanted a road bridge to connect with Southwick, a joint project was approved on the same principles as Robert Stephenson's High Level Bridge in Newcastle. The designer was Charles Augustus Harrison (1848–1916), nephew to Thomas Harrison who had assisted Stephenson with the Newcastle bridge in 1850. He was NER engineer for the Northern Section. The masonry approaches were constructed by Mitchell Brothers and the central span was erected by Sir William Arrol and Co., both of Glasgow. The bridge was built from both sides of the river simultaneously. During the construction process a gap of 1¼in occurred between the two halves of the central span, but this eventuality had been anticipated in the engineers' calculations. As predicted, rising temperatures caused the steel to expand, and the two sides met at around noon on 15 October 1908. The ends were quickly bolted together, and the rocker bearings at either end of the span, which allowed for the expansion and contraction of the steelwork, were released. Arrol and Co. had been involved in the construction of the Forth Bridge by the same method. In fact the central span of the Queen Alexandra Bridge was only 3¾ft longer than that of the Forth Bridge, but weighed three times as much. The excess weight meant that open-work towers had to be constructed on top of the stone piers and tied back with steel plate ties. These acted as cantilevers to support the two halves of the span as they extended from either side of the river. The total length of the bridge was 1560ft and the final cost was £450,000. The principal director of the construction was A.S. Biggart, managing director of Arrol and Co.

107 The Queen Alexandra Bridge was designed by Charles Harrison and constructed by Sir William Arrol and Co., 1908–09.

The bridge is raised on monumental sandstone piers, Piranesian in scale. These stand upon footings of Norwegian granite. Round-headed arches are formed in each pier, their soaring proportions and severity providing a glimpse of the architectural sublime. The piers are built of rock-faced stone to emphasise their strength and the top of each is treated as a gigantic Doric capital. The bridge itself has a latticed structure resembling a simple box-girder. The central span is hog-backed in form and 330ft long. A road bridge was enclosed within the structure and a rail bridge originally ran above. The bridge was opened on 10 June 1909 by the Earl of Durham on behalf of Alexandra, Queen Consort to Edward VII. The railway link was very short-lived, being abandoned in 1921 and leaving a road bridge that could not be easily improved to meet changing traffic conditions.[251] Having been built for coal traffic, the bridge is much stronger than it needs to be: 2,600 tons of steel were used in its construction, making it the heaviest bridge in Britain at the time. A fragment of the approaching rail viaduct survives to the north, with five epic-scaled arches in rock-faced red sandstone from Dumfries.

Tramways

Railways transformed Sunderland's transport links with its hinterland and with the rest of the country: tramways did the same within the town. The addition of tram services between the town centre and the suburbs had immediate benefits for work and leisure. Councils were not permitted to run tram systems directly, but they were permitted to encourage companies to do so. The Sunderland Tramways Company was established in 1878 and the first route, from Monkwearmouth to Roker, was running on 28 April 1879 with a flat fare of 2*d*. The London-based engineer J. Kincaid planned and supervised the laying of the tracks,[252] but the service was limited by a shortage of horses and by a lack of capital to fund extensions as demand for the service grew. As a result, when the opportunity arose in 1896 the Corporation bought out the company and operated the trams as a municipal service.[253] This coincided with the move to electric trams, which had begun elsewhere in the country; and as the Corporation had opened its first generating station in 1895 they were keen to upgrade the network. This process of electrification was planned and executed by the borough surveyor, R.S. Rounthwaite, together with the newly appointed borough electrical engineer, John Snell (1869–1938). It was originally intended to hold a competition for a new power station, but Snell announced that he had already produced a design. Despite some objections, the lighting committee decided that staging a competition would be an unnecessary expense and a waste of time.[254] Snell and J.W. Moncur designed and built the power station on ★Hylton Road in 1902 and ★Hendon Power Station in 1904, while Rounthwaite laid out the tracks and overhead cables. This work was continued by Rounthwaite's successor, Moncur.[255]

The Tramways Committee built a ★Headquarters Building at the Wheatsheaf (1903–05), with a very distinctive Baroque tower. The building was three storeys tall with a strong vertical emphasis, culminating in a series of triangular gables. The tower was an original composition with clock-faces around a hexagonal stage below a domed cupola. The building was designed by F.E. Coates (b.1873), who had also designed ★tram depots at the Wheatsheaf and on Hylton Road in 1903.[256] Coates was born at No. 5 The Craiglands in Sunderland. He was educated at the Grange School and articled to John Eltringham (1886–90) before travelling in Europe, where he made sketching tours. He was in practice from 1894 and joined Harry Barnes in partnership from 1895 to *c*.1902. Coates had a brief but flourishing career in his home town after winning the competition for the Shire Hall in Durham, but he chose to become assistant education architect to Durham County Council from 1908, working under William Rushworth.[257] Coates was a founder and committee member of Sunderland Antiquarian Society, and published an article on 'Old Sunderland'.

The tramway system was one of the largest undertakings of the council, yet it was largely taken for granted as it was extended throughout the town. Its impact in allowing working men to live at some distance from their employment was substantial, and it allowed estates to be built in parts of the town previously inhabited by the middle classes, as with the Little Egypt estate.[258]

6

Domestic Buildings

The most pressing factor in the history of Sunderland in the nineteenth century was the relentless rise in population. From a figure of 26,511 in 1801, the number of inhabitants rose nearly seven times to 182,260 in 1901.[259] These figures conceal differences in growth rates in the different parishes and at different periods within the century, but the ongoing rise presented the town with constant demands to build homes and facilities required for all these people. As a result the number of building firms listed in directories rose from only three in 1822 to sixty-six in 1900.[260] A similar pattern affected architects' firms, which increased from only one in 1822 to seventeen in 1902.[261] As in the rest of the country it was a good time to be an architect, with so much building work being undertaken. This was reflected in the growing awareness of the need for proper training and standards within the profession. Of all the demands for buildings, the one that was most urgent was the need to provide accommodation for the increasing population. Domestic architecture in Sunderland is very varied, ranging from the luxurious mansions of Victorian industrialists to the humble dwellings of the town's workforce.

Housing the Middle Class

Traditionally, the provision of housing had been largely the province of builders working from pattern books and using well-established practices rather than of architects, who were involved only with the grandest houses for the richest clients. This pattern was true in Sunderland, at least in the early part of the century. The middle classes had the resources and the opportunity to make choices about where they would live in the town and in what sort of houses. They moved away from the riverside in Sunderland parish in the eighteenth century, and that process continued in the nineteenth as they moved increasingly into Bishopwearmouth parish, especially onto the 19 acre Fawcett Estate. This land was an undeveloped area between the two parishes and opposite Wearmouth Bridge, the building of which had substantially increased its value; it was therefore a prime site for development.

William Jamieson, agent to John Fawcett, laid out the estate in 1810–14, and it was he who determined the grid pattern and the width of the streets, which made Fawcett Street so much wider than the others. Building did not take place immediately or rapidly, and by 1820 only five houses were recorded in directories. Robert Robson's map of 1827 shows only twelve houses, all at the north end.[262] Building in the other streets – John, Frederick and Foyle Streets – continued into the 1850s, although Pevsner dated the houses by their design as neo-Greek of c.1830, which shows that the development was rather out of date by national standards.[263]

The name of Bartholomew Dowell is most associated with the building of these houses. He was a builder based in Norfolk Street and his brother Richard (1762–1843), who was surveyor to the Improvement Commissioners, may have assisted him.[264] The development consisted of substantial terraced houses with rateable values of £25–30 per annum, comprising three reception rooms, two kitchens and eight bedrooms arranged over three floors and a half-basement in Fawcett Street. Smaller properties were built in the other streets. The overall design models were the terraces of Bath, London and Edinburgh of the previous century, which sought to achieve their architectural effect by massing the houses into larger units of building. These terraces had been largely built by builder developers, and Dowell fitted this pattern until he was bankrupted in 1843. Other builders, like Joseph Potts, Thomas Pratt and G.A. Middlemiss, who all had aspirations to become architects, also built on the estate, especially in the later phases.[265]

By 1842 John, Frederick and Foyle Streets were laid out in a strict grid pattern with uniformly Neoclassical terraces. These terraces can be aligned with the Greek Revival tradition. In the second half of the eighteenth century architects began to take a particular interest in the architecture of Ancient Greece, which was older and more severe than that of Rome. With the stagnation of the Turkish Ottoman Empire, Greece became more accessible to travellers. In 1751–54 the architects James Stuart (1713–88) and Nicholas Revett (1720–1804) made a tour of Greece, measuring and sketching Greek ruins. They published the four-volume study *Antiquities of Athens* in 1762, and this became a principal sourcebook on the subject, helping to fuel the Greek Revival. The severe Greek style was popular in the North of England, a prime example being Penshaw Monument (1844), which was based on the Temple of Hephaestus in Athens. This was designed by John (1787–1852) and Benjamin Green (c.1811–58) as a monument to John Lambton, Earl of Durham, and provided a glimpse of Arcadia amid the colliery-strewn landscapes of County Durham. The influence of such projects filtered down to domestic architecture.

The houses on the Fawcett Estate were intended for professional middle-class families, and most have basements for servants. John Street is the widest after Fawcett Street itself and the terraces are designed on a grander scale than its neighbours. The houses are three or five bays wide. Each has a doorcase with Greek Doric columns supporting an entablature, which has a frieze of anthemion motifs [Fig 108]. In most cases the doors fold inwards to form the reveals of the doorcase. The steps leading up to the door are lined with cast-iron railings. Some houses break from the pure austerity of Greek Revival design and have Tuscan pilasters or columns around the door. Moving east, Foyle Street is not as grand as John Street, but it has retained its road surface of granite setts and conveys some of the elegance these streets must have had when first built. Foyle Street was completed in about 1842 and is lined with terraces boasting Greek Doric columns. Each house has two storeys and a basement. The doorcases have pilasters and entablatures, some with Greek key motifs, others with anthemion friezes. A number of houses stand out. No. 3 is a detached house with a Doric doorcase. No. 13 is an end house built in about 1850, and is larger than the others. The doorcase has fully rounded Doric columns instead of pilasters. No. 14 was built in about 1840. It has a panelled door and, in common with many nineteenth-century doors in Sunderland, the central panels are circular. The entablature is supported on fluted Doric pilasters.

The problems of the Mowbray Estate south of Building Hill were resolved by a private Act of Parliament in 1840, which allowed land to be sold by G.I. Mowbray's executors at £600 per acre. Burdon Road was completed in 1839. This gave direct access to the town and made a new area available for superior housing.[266] At that time the only housing in the area was Ashburn House and West Hendon House; these were occupied by the

108　A Neoclassical doorcase in John Street.

109 Ashburn House was built in about 1835 by the banker Edward Backhouse.

Backhouse brothers, who ran the family bank in Sunderland [Fig 109]. The initial plan, involving extensions of existing roads to build crescents close to the town and villas in 2 acre plots beyond Building Hill, was designed by the Newcastle practice of John Green and his son Benjamin in 1841, but it failed to come to fruition.[267] The later scheme was to sell significant plots of land and allow the purchasers to develop them either for their own occupation or as a speculative venture. John and Benjamin Green were retained as architects, and any proposals had to meet their approval on behalf of the executors. As a result the first large houses built were both by the Greens. Nicholson House in Mowbray Road was designed in a Tudor Gothic style in 1850–51 for Alderman William Nicholson, who had a successful business in copper and other ships' metalware [Fig 110]. The house was built of ashlar on an L-shaped plan, although brick additions were later built at the rear. The garden front is two storeys high, and a full-height bay window projects from the third bay under a gabled peak, echoed in the form of miniature gablets above the windows. Each gable ends with an obelisk finial. The entrance is housed within a Tudor arch with foliated carving thriving in the spandrels. An oriel window juts out above the entrance, and the supporting bracket has carved rose, thistle and shamrock motifs signifying England, Scotland and Ireland. A stepped chimney thrusts out from the second gable. At the rear, a buttressed projection emerges from the fourth bay, containing a Tudor arch and gable. The steeply pitched roof has two parallel ridges and a cross ridge, with tall chimneys rising from the junction.

110 Nicholson House, Mowbray Road, by John and Benjamin Green, 1850–51.

Bede Tower in Ryhope Road was built in 1851 for Anthony John Moore, solicitor, chairman of the Gas Company and Mayor of Sunderland from 1854–55 [Fig 111]. It was designed in the Italian Renaissance style, adapted to convey the domesticity befitting a private villa. The house consists of a two-storey block with a five-stage tower. The main block is subtly articulated with keystones and shallow rustication. A two-storey bay window projects from the second bay, offsetting symmetry. A pierced balustrade runs around the first floor, where a balcony juts out, supported on moulded brackets. The rightmost bay recedes behind the plane of the building and is articulated with sharply defined quoins. To achieve an appropriately domestic character, the architects included prominent overhanging eaves. The diminutive belvedere tower is comparable to that of Osborne House (1845–51).[268]

A.J. Moore had hired the Greens to design a scheme for nineteen houses on the same site, but this came to nothing.[269] However, Moore developed the site using a local architect, G.A. Middlemiss, who was making the transition from builder to architect at this time. The gated roads of St Bede's Terrace and Park Place East and West, together with Douro Terrace and the new streets of Peel Street, Nelson Street, St Vincent Street and Salem Street (intended for a lower social group), were all designed by Middlemiss in the 1850s. While he designed some of the houses, other architects and builders were probably also involved. They continued the tradition of terraced housing for the prosperous professional classes, though now with heavier, more Italianate detailing and

111 Bede Tower by John and Benjamin Green, 1851.

in many cases with front gardens. Douro Terrace was lined with superior terraces, each house consisting of three bays, with two storeys and a basement [Fig 112]. Like the houses on the Fawcett Estate, each property has a Greek Revival doorcase with Doric columns, but the addition of bay windows distinguishes these later houses. At Park Place the doorcases are somewhat richer, with Ionic columns and dentils, and the first-floor windows have projecting cornices supported on scrolled brackets. The houses on St Bede's Terrace have doorcases with three-quarter Corinthian columns.

These designs were much repeated through the Mowbray Estate up to the 1880s, when Middlemiss laid out The Elms for houses worth £1,200, and into Ashbrooke[270] [Fig 113]. They also established the pattern of developing with private gated roads, which gave greater privacy and may also have been a means of avoiding the by-laws regarding minimum widths and proper drainage in public roads. From 1855 to 1863 Middlemiss served as a Conservative councillor for Bridge Ward. He was opposed to the progressive policies of Candlish and Williams and had several clashes with the town clerk, John Snowball. He reserved his main antipathy for the public health and building regulations, as these limited his activities as a developer. To avoid these rules he often built outside the borough boundary where the legislation did not operate. When he built within the boundaries he did not seek approval, as the penalties were not sufficient deterrent. This was significant, as about half the development in the 1880s was on

112 Douro Terrace by G.A. Middlemiss, 1850s.

113 The Elms West by G.A. Middlemiss, 1880s.

Middlemiss's land. His extensive estates in Hendon, built in conjunction with J.C. Tone, were known for their unsanitary character, being a subject of comment even in the national journals. His most spectacular conflict was over St Bede's Terrace. In this development the initial building took place before the Sunderland Improvement Act was passed, meaning that no permission was needed, but the second phase in the 1860s was seen by the council as infringing the regulations. Middlemiss objected on behalf of his client, A.J. Moore, and the case eventually went to the Court of Chancery. The decision went against the council on the grounds that the whole development had been proposed before the Act, even though construction had been delayed.

The area to the south of the town became highly desirable. At the same time Fawcett Street was becoming less attractive, as traffic from the bridge could pass along the street on its way to Ryhope and Stockton. Development continued, and the area that came to be known as Ashbrooke became the most favoured site for middle-class residences in the town. The most striking development was on the Grange Estate, where ★St George's Square was built in 1855–56. This was an exclusive square with gates and a central garden area. The overall design was by Martin Greener (1818–89), although the houses were built by different builders for different clients.[271] Greener was born in Hebburn and received architectural training with John Dobson in Newcastle. He commenced practice in Sunderland in 1852. Among his pupils were John Tillman and Henry Grieves of South Shields. Greener's practice was a general one, but he was a prolific designer of houses in the mid-1850s, creating an Italianate terrace style, in brick with stone dressings and bay windows, which is common on the Mowbray Estate. His major building was the Primitive Methodist Chapel in Hetton-le-Hole (1856–58), which has a plain exterior but a magnificent interior with sweeping gallery. St George's Square has been demolished, so the best remaining example of this style of housing is The Esplanade, in which each house was built separately.

The Esplanade (1853–60) is among the most exclusive streets in Sunderland. It is set back from busy Stockton Road and screened by attractive private gardens. The complex consists of nine houses with lavish decoration. Each has a rusticated basement, doorcases with consoles and an entablature with modillions and paterae. The windows have cornices, and the eaves are supported on brackets projecting from the roofline. The first house to be built was for the shipbuilder Samuel Austin. Esplanade West, running opposite, is an echo of the main block but on a more modest scale. Greener was the architect of at least three houses in The Esplanade in 1855.[272] Greener is also shown in the Building Committee Minutes of the 1850s as designing a great deal of housing both to the east and north of Building Hill, including Grange Crescent, as well as further out on the West Hendon Estate in ★Cumberland Terrace and Cedars Terrace. Grange Crescent (1851–55) is an elegant terrace arcing around the corner into Stockton Road [Fig 114]. The houses are in an austere neo-Greek style with pilasters to the doorcases. Thomas Oliver, who was working in Sunderland before returning to Newcastle to establish one of the biggest practices in the North East, was also planning estates and designing houses in the district.[273] The process continued along Tunstall Road, with developments such as Humbledon View by Martin Greener in 1885 and the gated squares like Holmlands Park, designed by Frank Caws in 1896.[274] There were also houses for the less well off who wanted to live in a favoured area, as with Argyll Square, designed by Middlemiss in 1865–70.[275]

114 Grange Crescent by Martin Greener, 1851–55.

115 Ashbrooke House by Thomas Moore, 1864. (Image courtesy of Sunderland Museum)

While the building of terraces of this type continued through the Ashbrooke area, there were also some individual houses designed for the wealthiest inhabitants. A new house for the rector of St Michael's Church, Bishopwearmouth, was needed, as the existing one beside the church was deemed too large for convenience and the site opposite the church on High Street West had development value. John Dobson, who had extended the church and completed several other commissions for the Anglicans in the town, designed St Michael's House, a hard red-brick Gothic house in Gray Road (1858). This was quite unlike any other Dobson house, and incorporated the grand staircase from the previous rectory.[276] The glassmaker James Hartley commissioned Thomas Moore to design ★Ashbrooke House in 1864 [Fig 115]. The two-storey classical house had a large portico at the entrance and round-headed windows in the first floor. An apsidal projection emerged at one side, with multiple stained glass windows demonstrating Hartley's pre-eminence in the Sunderland glass trade. The interior reportedly had a spacious staircase and decorous plaster ceilings, making it one of the finest houses ever built in the town. Ashbrooke House was acquired by the Jesuits in 1933 and renamed Corby Hall. The house was converted into a retreat for Catholics and the polygonal apse became a chapel [Fig 116]. The building was eventually demolished in the 1970s to make way for flats.

Park House in Mowbray Road was built by an unknown architect in 1864 as a large double-fronted house with classical detailing.[277] The Briery was built in about 1870 in Ashbrooke Road for the ropemaker Hiram Craven. This was designed in a domestic Tudor style with projecting gables at either end and three bay windows emerging from the façade. The house was executed in red brick with stone dressings. Terracotta ridge tiles and a variegated slate roof enhanced its vibrant colour. The house was subsumed into St Aidan's RC School in 1936.

Large houses were built on the edge of the town at Ashbrooke Cross. In 1871 Frank Caws moved the classical Cresswell House

116 The apse at Ashbrooke House was later converted into a Roman Catholic chapel. (Image courtesy of Sunderland Museum)

117 Ashbrooke Tower by G.A. Middlemiss, 1875.

from the Thornhill area and re-erected it as Rosedene, so that new streets of
smaller houses could be laid out on the original site. In 1875 G.A. Middlemiss
designed the vast Gothic mansion Ashbrooke Tower as his retirement home.[278]
[Fig 117]. He lived here in his last years and was cared for by his daughter after
the death of his second wife, Anne. The house is built of red brick and boasts a
castellated tower above the entrance, a medieval fantasy recreated in suburban
Sunderland. In Thornhill there was development after 1875 and 1876 when the
estate was auctioned off. Martin Greener laid out Thornhill Park for William
Botterill with sites for 'costly mansions occupied by the elite of the town'.
J. and T. Tillman built such a mansion for J.S. Wilson in a style derived from
late medieval domestic architecture.[279] This process continued until 1914,
the best example being Hammerton Hall in Gray Road [Fig 118]. Built as a
modern villa in the leafy suburb of Ashbrooke, the house was designed by the
talented local architect C.A. Clayton Greene. Hammerton Hall was inspired
by Edgar Wood's design for Upmeads, a country house in Stafford (1906).
Unconventional in form, Upmeads is built around a courtyard. Its most
remarkable feature is a shallow receding curve in the main frontage, where
the entrance is emphasised by a strip of masonry running up to the roofline.
Like Upmeads, Hammerton Hall exhibits a concave façade and juxtaposes
brick wall surfaces with a vertical strip of stone in the central bay. A window
above the entrance is composed of thick stone mullions, recalling the robust
simplicity of Arts and Crafts buildings. The stone centrepiece features a low

relief in 'stripped classical' form. Framing the door, the porch is an expressive design, with curved wooden beams assembled into a bold structure. Arrayed along the roofline, the chimneys are built of brick in heavy block-like forms.

Unlike Upmeads, the side wings are not built in a continuous line but are at right angles to each other. In this respect Hammerton Hall was possibly influenced by The Barn (1896), a seaside house in Exmouth, Devon, designed by the Arts and Crafts architect E.S. Prior. This house was based on a butterfly plan, in which the wings embrace the entrance courtyard, forming a suntrap. The Barn featured in Hermann Muthesius's study of English

118 Hammerton Hall, Gray Road, by C.A. Clayton Greene, 1914.

domestic architecture, *Das Englische Haus* (1904), and had considerable influence in Britain and on the Continent. Significantly, Greene's church of St Gabriel had been inspired by Prior's radical design for St Andrew's at Roker, confirming that Greene was aware of Prior's work. Hammerton Hall is therefore an amalgam of two of the most advanced domestic buildings of the period and a testament to Greene's knowledge of progressive architectural trends. Born in London, he was the son of the Revd W.E. Freeman Greene. He was articled to Benjamin Simpson of Newcastle and entered practice in partnership with H.T.D. Hedley in 1899. He worked in Sunderland for the whole of his career, enjoying a varied practice. Domestic architecture was a strong focus of his work, and in this field he was influenced by Sir Edwin Lutyens (1869–1944), whom he greatly admired. He was also skilled in ecclesiastical architecture and published a book, *Churches and their Building*, which gave practical advice on church design and advocated Gothic as the most suitable style for Anglican buildings. The book contains an account of the building of St Gabriel's Church, Sunderland. Greene was an active member of Christ Church, Ashbrooke, and a processional cross was given in his memory after he died. He served in both World Wars as a valuer for the War Department, but retired from architecture in 1937.

For the wealthiest citizens there was still the option of moving beyond the edge of the town and building a country house in substantial grounds. Two members of the Doxford shipbuilding family did this: Theodore Doxford at

Grindon Hall by J. and T. Tillman (1885) and Robert Doxford at Silksworth Hall by Hedley and Greene (1905).²⁸⁰ Silksworth Hall is a free Jacobean-style mansion built of red brick with sandstone dressings. The bulk is split into three wide gables, the central bay receding behind a classical loggia with Ionic pilasters. Flanking the loggia, semicircular drums project beneath hemispherical roofs. Stepped chimney-stacks emerge from the outer gables and terminate in strong octagonal chimneys. The central gable is surmounted by a dragon finial. Turning the corner, the west elevation has two gabled bays flanking a Jacobean-style blind arcade and oriel window. The rear has projecting canted bays and a first-floor balcony. The building was used as a hotel for many years. Hedley and Greene's partnership ended in 1905, whereupon Hedley worked independently and designed a number of public houses. Greene went on to design a series of expressive buildings informed by fashionable architectural trends.

The most distinctive of the superior houses built beyond the edge of town is Langham Tower (1886–91), a suburban mansion built for William Adamson, a trader in ships' stores [Plate 14]. The architect was William Milburn, whose father's office was located next door to Adamson's in Nile Street. This was his first major commission, and he clearly enjoyed the freedom of a substantial budget of £5,000 and a client who wanted his house to make a mark on his community. A rambling composition anchored around its remarkable tower, Langham Tower is complex in its massing and bewildering in its variety of detail. The main bulk is executed in red brick with dressings of sandstone, but it abounds with half-timbered gables and decorative motifs drawn from a range of styles. The tower thrusts out at the west and terminates with a diminutive but fully formed gable. A deep recess cut into the base of the tower encloses the entrance. A colossal chimney of moulded brick is built alongside, giving prominence to the narrow frontage. On the chimney is a terracotta panel depicting a lion in profile; a banner above reads 'Semper Paratus' (Always Ready). Turning the corner, a wider elevation rises at the south, with three projecting bays of varying form: a square block with overhanging gable is succeeded by a canted bay, before an octagonal turret completes the group. This is crowned with a short spire recessed behind mock battlements. The red-brick execution and extensive use of terracotta ornament suggest an awareness of the burgeoning Queen Anne movement, particularly the potted-sunflower motif on the exterior.

The house unfolds as a series of carefully constructed views that proclaim the wealth and status of the owner. The tunnel-like entrance porch is framed by a rich Tudor arch carved with strikingly naturalistic leaf and animal forms. The wide doorway features large panes of bevelled glass permitting a view of the opulent interior, which is lined with rich wood panelling. A staircase rises around three sides, and at the foot stands a statue of an armoured warrior brandishing a gas-lit torch. Dominating the hall is a vast window.

Executed by Atkinson Brothers of Newcastle, the window features twelve stained-glass panels celebrating the technological and cultural achievements of Victorian Britain [Fig 119]. Adjoining the hall is the baronial dining room, a large chamber with a lustrous ceiling of pressed paper and copper. The room is dominated by a marble fireplace set within a rich Tudor arch. Hunting motifs and stained glass panels depicting medieval knights emphasise the wealth, confidence and sense of ancestry of the building.

Langham Tower was part of the much wider Domestic Revival in architecture. Figures such as Philip Webb (1831–1915) and Norman Shaw began to explore the legacy of English domestic architecture, reviving styles such as Tudor and Queen Anne, both of which are in evidence at

119 A figure of an armoured warrior brandishing a torch. The stained-glass window behind celebrates the technological and cultural achievements of Victorian Britain.

Langham Tower. Queen Anne was a newly fashionable style that spread out from London. Principally used in the affluent neighbourhoods of the West End, the style flourished 'because it satisfied all the latest aspirations of the English middle classes'.[281] Queen Anne became a mainstay of the Aesthetic Movement with its cult of art for art's sake. The somewhat frivolous nature of the style matched the new taste for beauty uncomplicated by moral precepts or theology. Like Queen Anne, the Tudor style was a key component of the Domestic Revival. Indeed, the eminent architect J.J. Stevenson (1831–1908) argued that the Tudor style was ideally suitable for domestic purposes: 'For the charm of homeliness nothing can surpass the houses of the Tudor age, with their mullioned windows and oak carving, and we can only feebly imitate the sumptuousness and elegance of those of the Renaissance of Francis I or of our own Jacobean.'[282]

In particular, Langham Tower is derived from the very large houses of Norman Shaw, buildings that combined a knowledge of English domestic architecture with the latest technical innovations. Cragside, the romantic country mansion of Lord Armstrong, was a local example that Milburn would have known, and Shaw's designs (1883–85) were extensively illustrated in the architectural press. Certain elements, such as the gabled tower, octagonal turret and inglenook fireplace, are direct quotations from Cragside. Langham Tower possesses its share of unique features, however. Hunting motifs proliferate, including the heads of wild boars and lions, which project from the black-painted eaves. Swirling leaf forms in the external plasterwork add an Art Nouveau flourish to the very English half-timbering. If anything, the contrasts of style, colour and material are even more vibrant in Langham Tower. An imitation of Cragside it may be, but Langham Tower achieves the same eccentricity and exuberance on a reduced scale, and this is all the more apparent in its suburban setting. William Milburn subsequently went on to create the town's most important architectural practice with his brother Thomas, which designed many important buildings in Sunderland and across the country, but this is an exuberant young man's design, full of inventive detail. It was not long used as a house as it required too many servants to function comfortably, and after 1919 it became Sunderland Teacher Training College.[283]

While the wealthy inhabitants of the town were happy to live south of Mowbray Park, there was a greater reluctance to build on the other prime site in the town – the seafront. This was partly because there was a single landowner, Sir Hedworth Williamson of Whitburn Hall, who controlled most of the land. Williamson was involved with many other developments of a commercial nature that were absorbing his time and resources. Another disadvantage was that the route back to the centre of town was longer, passed through industrial and working-class areas and required the crossing of the toll bridge over the Wear. So while other seaside towns rushed to exploit the healthy air and sea views, Sunderland declined to develop its seafront until quite late. One attempt was made in 1840–41 when a hotel, public baths and a terrace of holiday homes were built at Roker, served by the new Roker Baths Road. As was usual with a Williamson development, the architect was John Dobson, and he worked in a conventional classical style to produce a well-mannered terrace.[284] Joseph Potts and Son provided plans for further building around Roker Terrace in 1869, but more extensive building was restricted by Roker Ravine, which prevented wheeled traffic proceeding along the coast and so forced all traffic to move inland and on to Whitburn.[285] Williamson solved this problem by offering Roker Dene, which was unsuitable for building, to the Corporation as a public park on condition that they built a bridge over the ravine. When this was achieved with Potts's utilitarian bridge design in 1880 and the opening of the park in the same year,[286] the development potential of Roker and Seaburn could finally be realised. Terraces of richly detailed houses were built around the park in the Rock Lodge Estate by Potts in 1884 and later in Park Parade in the years up to 1900.[287] Along the coast a few large houses were built, but the bulk of the development was for white-collar workers who were able to use the trams to get to work each day. Frank Caws produced a large-scale estate design for Seaburn in 1901. This was not built as planned, but it provided the basis for the subsequent development of the area at the eastern end of Sea Road.[288] There are also examples of early semi-detached houses on

120 The white- and red-brick houses of Viewforth Terrace were designed by an
unknown architect in the 1870s.

Seaside Lane, designed by G.T. Brown (1866–1922) in 1903.[289] Some building
occurred along Newcastle Road, including impressive fiercely Gothic houses
in Viewforth Terrace. These were built in white and red brick by an unknown
architect. Dating from the 1870s, they are of a style not to be found elsewhere
in the town [Fig 120].

Housing the Working Class

Where did the workers of Sunderland live, the people who created the wealth
on which the town was built? The working class had little say as to where they
lived or in what style of housing. Their houses were fitted in when the wealthy
and industry had selected their preferred sites. Speculative builders could then
build near to new employment opportunities, and the workers could walk to
the shipyard, mine or dock from their homes close by. Indeed, the poorest of
them had to live in adaptations and infillings of the existing housing stock.
This produced the overcrowded slums that were all their incomes permitted
them to rent. No architect was involved with these desperate solutions to the
housing problem. Nor were architects keen to design new housing for the
working class until there were changes in the legislative framework intended
to tackle the worst excesses of bad health and slum housing. The Sunderland
Improvement Act of 1851 was primarily intended to allow the Corporation

to take over the powers and assets of the Improvement Commissioners and to unify local government in the town. It also incorporated the provisions of the 1848 Public Health Act and applied them to Sunderland. Among the provisions was the appointment of a medical officer of health and a borough surveyor. The surveyor was to enforce the newly written building regulations and to advise his Building Committee as to whether plans for new buildings met these regulations. Although the regulations dealt only with sanitary provision and basic minimum requirements of space and light, they were the first step in establishing appropriate standards of housing. Crucially, they required a plan to be drawn and submitted before approval to build could be granted. The effect of these regulations was diminished by builders developing sites outside the borough boundary in New Hendon, where they were free to build to whatever standards they chose. As a result mortality rates rose in Hendon while they dropped within the borough.[290] While builders continued to dominate this field, architects became involved in the drawing of these plans, especially for the layout of estates, and so became involved in the design of housing for the ordinary family.

Most towns soon found a design of house that would meet the building regulations, could be built relatively easily and for a price that matched the level of rents that were available. These houses were attractive to investors, who bought them to rent to workers and their families. Some of these designs were widely to be found: back-to-backs in the West Riding, tunnel backs in the East Midlands, tenements in Glasgow and Tyneside flats around Newcastle, but Sunderland produced a design that is virtually unique to the town – the Sunderland cottage [Fig 121].

121 Sunderland cottages, Abingdon Street, High Barnes, by W. and T.R. Milburn.

These single-storey terraces
seem to date originally from about
1840 and they were built in all
areas of the town up to the First
World War, and in some areas even
later. There is debate about where
the form came from and why it
was adopted in Sunderland and
nowhere else, but it has remained a
style that has satisfied housing needs
to the present day.[291] Its supporters
have emphasised the degree of
privacy obtained by allocating each
property its own back yard and
sanitary facilities, and by having
too little space to encourage the
introduction of lodgers. Similarly,
the through ventilation of houses
with front and back doors gave
an advantage over back-to-backs,
and the universal provision of
back lanes made for easy access by
service providers like nightsoil men
and refuse collectors. Detractors
have noted the monotony of the
terraced streets and the relatively
large amount of land needed for
each property. A pair of back-to-
backs required about 50 square
yards of land, while two cottages

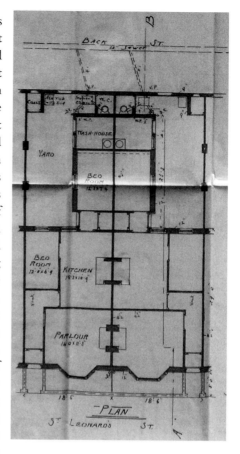

122 Plan of two cottages in St Leonard's
Street, Hendon, by H.E. Robinson,
1901. (Image courtesy of Tyne and Wear
Archives Service)

separated by their back lane needed some 146 square yards.[292] Over the years
the design of the cottages developed, and some streets show several different
types within a terrace. The main improvement was to build them with
double frontages and a central doorway, which permitted two bedrooms
and two living rooms, with the kitchen as an off-shoot in the yard. Bay
windows and small front areas to set the entrance back from the street
were often introduced, largely as cosmetic features [Fig 122]. Occasionally
dormers were added to allow use of the loft space for additional bedrooms.
This gave the cottage a degree of flexibility that made it attractive to a
range of potential occupiers. A good number of these occupiers were also
owners of the property, as a result of the activities of small building societies
who sponsored the building of small estates for well-paid skilled men in
the shipyards, who could afford the repayments and had sufficiently secure

employment to be a reasonable credit risk. While Daunton suggests that overall owner occupancy in Sunderland in the 1890s was at 27.3 per cent, significantly higher than other towns, Longstaffe has shown that in the streets in his study the figures could be higher: 50 per cent in Ridley Terrace and 86.6 per cent in Tower Street in an earlier period.[293] An example of such a building society scheme was that planned by the Universal Building Society in the Valley of Love in 1865. Designed by John Tillman and built by J.C. Tone, houses to a total value of £35,000 were to be built in Mainsforth Terrace, Tower Street and Hendon Burn Avenue over three years. These were wide streets with good sewerage and sites earmarked for churches within the estate. The scheme demonstrated that cottages could cater for the aspirations of the skilled working man.[294]

Close analysis reveals that many cottages emulate recognisable architectural styles, albeit crudely. Style is rarely consistent throughout an entire street, because the cottages were usually built by different builders. Builders operated on limited budgets and could not afford elaborate stylistic details: it is likely that they chose decorative elements from published sources such as pattern books or suppliers' catalogues. Much of Britain's terraced housing was designed in the classical idiom. In most cases the Sunderland cottage follows this precedent and displays modest classical details. For example, the lintels over doors and windows emulate classical architraves. Some streets have a row of projecting bricks just below the roofline, echoing the dentilled cornices that are common in classical ornament. A prime example is Dickens Street in Southwick. In common with most English terraced housing in the first half of the nineteenth century, then, the majority of Sunderland cottages fall broadly within the tradition of Neoclassicism. Later developments introduced a range of decorative detail. By the 1860s Gothic motifs had begun to permeate domestic architecture, and Gothic details are apparent in Ridley Terrace, Hendon, one of the earliest surviving streets, where several doors have rudimentary Gothic arches executed in brick [Fig 123]. Variegated designs occur in James Armitage Street in Southwick. Both these streets are now listed for their historic interest. Blackett Terrace is exceptional in being the only cottage street in Sunderland to have a gate at either end, with just a narrow footpath to access the front of the houses. This suggests that Blackett Terrace was conceived as a private road in order to circumvent the by-law stipulation that each street must be at least 30ft wide, or perhaps the fact that there were no houses opposite meant that the usual rules did not apply.

The earliest example of an architect planning a cottage estate that has come to light is Martin Greener at South Dock Street, Hendon, showing that he was prepared to design housing for all classes of the population.[295] But it was G.A. Middlemiss who was most active in the field. Given his conservative views when he was a town councillor, and his vehement opposition to public

123 Sunderland cottages, Ridley Terrace, 1860s.

health regulations, he took a strongly free market approach to building and so built on his own land in Hendon outside the Corporation's jurisdiction whenever possible. He had built up substantial wealth as an auctioneer, appraiser and owner of the Cornhill Brick Works in Southwick, apart from his architectural activities. Having started his career in the building firm of J.C. Tone, who built many of the cottages around Wearmouth Colliery, he was well placed to be a major developer in the town. In the 1870s he was building extensively in Hendon, and in the 1880s he laid out 350 houses in the Little Egypt estate off Villette Road and also an estate of 'superior' cottages on the Briery Vale estate off Tunstall Road[296] [Fig 124].

The role played by architects in the development of Sunderland cottages is a complex issue. Historians have suggested that cottages were built by speculative builders without the aid of professional architects.[297] Nevertheless, recent research has established that the majority of Sunderland cottages were designed by the town's prominent architects.[298] The Milburns designed the 'ABC streets' in High Barnes (Abingdon, Barnard, Eastfield and Guisborough Streets), as well as Kitchener Street, Nora Street, Hawarden Crescent, Queen's Crescent, Tanfield Street and Hampden Road. They also designed seventeen cottages in Broadsheath Terrace and nine in Ancona Street. On his own account, William Milburn produced the designs for Chester Street, Co-operative Terrace, Grindon Terrace and Dene Street.

124 Sunderland cottages, Cairo Street, Hendon, by H.E. Robinson, *c*.1900.

Joseph Potts and Son were also prolific cottage designers; they provided the
designs for the 'Scottish streets' in Fulwell – Forfar, Inverness, Moray and
Roxburgh Streets. Most historians argue that Sunderland cottages ceased
to be built after 1910. In fact, substantial numbers were built into the 1920s
and 1930s. The vast majority of late examples were built under a scheme
entitled Housing Assistance to Private Enterprise, which was introduced
by the Housing Estate Act of 1923, in which private builders were given
subsidies to build houses. In Sunderland the subsidy was typically £100 per
block of houses. The largest concentration of new cottages occurred among
the 'Scottish streets' in Fulwell. Forfar Street was commenced in 1906,
but was extended in 1925, principally by the builders C.B. Carr and C.R.
Wills.[299] The building of Inverness Street had begun in 1899, but a further
forty-seven cottages were built between 1923 and 1926.[300] Moray Street was
built entirely between 1926 and 1933, mainly by C.B. Carr. All of these
new cottages were designed by Joseph Potts and Son. The north side of
Mafeking Street, comprising twenty-one cottages, was built by J.W. White
in 1924.[301] In Hendon, St Leonard's Street was extended between 1924 and
1928.[302] Even today, Sunderland cottages represent the backbone of working-
class communities across the city.

   Some builders created alternatives to the cottage. There are a few Tyneside
Flats in John Candlish Street and especially in Gladstone Street, though the
other streets in that particular development have cottages. Stansfield Street

has a very varied set of designs within the terraces. Where businesses built directly for their own workforce they followed the patterns they had already established. The North Eastern Railway built housing for many of its staff. William Bell, the company architect from 1877 to 1914, provided standard NER designs for houses in Lyndhurst Road, Pallion, and at Southwick. Joseph Potts supervised their construction.[303]

Speculative building firms were providing cottages across the town in Pallion, Southwick, north of Roker Avenue, between Hylton Road and Chester Road and especially Hendon, as new industrial developments provided a demand for housing in those areas. Some attempts were made to provide housing that might be seen as directly tackling the sanitary and health problems from which the town undoubtedly suffered. The largest scheme was pursued by Sir Hedworth Williamson in Monkwearmouth (1851–57). Williamson had already commissioned John Dobson to plan developments on Monkwearmouth Shore in conjunction with a new road to serve his new North Dock in 1835, but he was later to produce a much larger scheme.[304] His development on a ballast hill in *East House Field produced an estate of nine streets (Ann, Barrington, Bloomfield, Dame Dorothy, Dock, Hardwick, Mulgrave and Normanby Streets, as well as Milburn Place). There were also 400 houses intended for the workers based on the north bank of the river. John Dobson laid out the estate and designed two-storey houses with basements in a regular grid, which was viewed as a 'decided improvement on the domestic architecture of the neighbourhood', though it does not look very different from much workers' housing of the period. Provision was also made for the Corporation to build a *public bath and washhouse within the estate in 1853.[305] In other towns a common way of building superior dwellings for workers was through the Land Society Estate movement sponsored by the Liberal Party, which acquired sites and then built houses with a rateable value sufficient to gain the occupier a parliamentary vote. Although their motivation was primarily political they built better than average houses. Only one example in Sunderland has come to light. This was on the north side of Hylton Road, where Joseph Potts laid out an estate in 1852. It is not clear whether the subsequent development was actually completed by the Land Society.[306]

A common way to find designs for model houses was to organise competitions which would attract young architects to design improved houses within the budget set in the rules. This does not seem to have been widely attempted in Sunderland, but in 1872 the Corporation held a competition for houses to be built on cleared land. Sixty designs were received, and premiums were awarded to Thomas Oliver and John Tillman for two-storey designs. The Sunderland Dwelling Company erected some housing further down High Street East in Lucknow, Hartley, Havelock and Outram Streets. These were let as flats, but the Corporation did not seem to use the designs.[307] Another scheme on a larger scale was the redevelopment of Hartley's Glassworks after it closed in the 1890s. Here the architect, James Henderson, provided eighteen shops on Hylton Road, and in the streets behind built 205 houses on the 7 acre site, a density of thirty houses to the acre. On the other side of Hylton Road further shops and fifty-four houses were planned, the whole scheme to be built over five years.[308]

The driving force to improve housing conditions was the local authority. At that time they were actively involved with implementing the Sunderland Improvement Act of 1867, which gave them powers to demolish unsatisfactory housing and to replace it with model dwellings. In 1872 they were in the process of building James Williams Street, and yet they do not seem to have used their chosen house designs in that development. While they demolished much unsanitary housing, they built very few replacement properties and so did little to alleviate the housing problem. Fourteen two-storey houses (by an unknown designer) were built, but the bulk of the street was filled with a Board School, three chapels and a dispensary.[309] This first attempt by the council to improve housing failed to achieve a great deal. Other attempts were made in Roker Avenue that were rather more successful,[310] but the first real attempt at council housing was ★Harrison's Buildings, built under the provisions of the Housing of the Working Classes Act of 1890. Although the Hat Case and Fitters Row area was designated as unfit in 1892, it was not until 1896 that the architectural competition was won by M.B. Perry and Robert Angell of London, and it was 1904 before tenants had moved in after disputes over the design with the Local Government Board in London and delays in the building process. The architectural competition was for forty-two three-roomed and fifty-four two-roomed dwellings housing 468 people. Each was to include a bath. The assessor of the competition ruled out a number of plans incorporating external balcony walkways on the grounds that these had proved unpopular with flat-dwellers. Perry and Angell won the competition, but their plans were modified for reasons of economy. The baths were omitted and the accommodation was reduced to 325. In order to replace the accommodation demolished with an equivalent number of units, the design had to be for rather barrack-like tenements, which was a new development in Sunderland. The buildings were three storeys high and austere in design, but with oriel windows projecting at first-floor level. Because of the long time taken to build, few of the displaced families can have been rehoused in the new flats.[311] While this particular development may have been fraught with problems, it heralded what would be a major effort in council housing in the town throughout the twentieth century.

On the outskirts of Sunderland, but now within the city boundary, housing followed the pattern of the small mining villages of the county. New Tunstall (now Silksworth) was built following the winning of the pit in 1868 and is a classic mining village of 40 acres and 350 houses in nine streets completed by 1874. Overmen's houses of five rooms were sited separately from the main housing, as were those of the sinkers, and the remainder were of three different classes ranging from two rooms with pantry and yard to four ground-floor rooms. All were built to a uniform plan. The streets, named after the marquis's children, were well laid out and properly drained and the houses all had gardens, usually to the front. As this was a Londonderry pit, the layout and the detailed designs were probably by William Forster, Londonderry's architect and surveyor from about 1871 to 1895, who certainly did design community buildings in the village. These included the schools of 1876, a Primitive Methodist Chapel in 1877 and the Volunteer Drill Hall of 1883. As an experiment, twenty-six of the houses were built of cement.[312] Interestingly, the Rural District Council was ahead of Sunderland in the provision of council housing, with two schemes in Ryhope and Silksworth to provide a total of 120 dwellings with forty-eight flats, forty-eight five-room houses and twenty-four four-room houses at a total cost of £22,000. Designed and built in 1906–09 by Joseph Spain, they are typical council houses, taking their inspiration from schemes like Bournville in Birmingham.[313] Spain was born in Sunderland, the son of Jacob Spain, superintendent of the James Westoll shipping company. He was articled to T.R. Milburn from 1887 to 1892 and continued as his assistant. In 1894 he passed the Qualifying Examination second on the national listings and was nominated as Associate of the RIBA on 11 March 1895. He commenced private practice the same year in John Street, when Milburn joined his brother in partnership, and worked with G.T. Brown until about 1914.

Conclusion

Sunderland was transformed by the architects, engineers and builders of the eighteenth and nineteenth centuries. During this period the infrastructure of a modern industrial town was created in terms of street patterns and the provision of public utilities and transport routes. Into this infrastructure the buildings Sunderland needed in order to carry on its business and to make the town convenient for its inhabitants were introduced. This was largely achieved by architects based in the town. Most of them were not outstanding, though a few – Moore, Oliver, Caws and the Milburns – produced buildings of real merit that contributed much to the townscape. Several of the region's leading figures – Dobson, Johnson, Fowler, Hoskins, Pritchett and Hicks – also made a mark in the town, but few nationally important architects gained commissions. An exception was E.S. Prior who, at St Andrew's Church, Roker, designed the finest building in Sunderland. A good deal of Victorian development has been demolished or the buildings made over for new uses, but enough remains to give some idea of what the town was like in the nineteenth century.

Victorian Sunderland was proud and prosperous. The coal trade, shipbuilding and other industries generated wealth, and much of it was expended on building activity. The vast capital outlay required by the town's industries meant that extensive capital organisation was needed. Banks became integral to Sunderland's economy, and their importance was reflected in the richness of their designs. A number of palatial banks were erected on Fawcett Street, which emerged as the town's major financial axis. Some of these were designed by important national practitioners, such as John Gibson and C.R. Gribble, as part of vast branch networks for particular firms. Introducing the latest architectural styles to Sunderland, these buildings became highlights within the townscape and provided inspiration for local practitioners. Commercial enterprise also provided Sunderland with places of entertainment and leisure, including theatres, hotels, public houses, parks and sports grounds.

The most pressing factor in Sunderland's development was the need to provide accommodation for the increasing population. The wealthiest citizens were involved in laying out estates and building private villas, and to a large extent they determined what types of housing were adopted. The middle classes moved to elegant Neoclassical terraces on the Fawcett Estate until commercial development undermined its social exclusivity. Thereafter, the wealthier citizens built Italianate terraces and distinguished villas on the Mowbray Estate and in the affluent suburb of Ashbrooke. Conversely, working-class housing had to fit into the areas not claimed by the wealthy or by industry. Working-class housing was for the most part built by speculative builders rather than the Corporation or philanthropists. At first the majority of workers lived close to bases of industry, but as time went on expanding transport networks made it possible to live further from the workplace. By the late nineteenth century many skilled artisans were able to follow the middle class to the more affluent districts, and in this they were aided by the availability of Sunderland cottages, a distinctive form of workers' housing that allowed well-paid artisans to emulate the living standards of the middle class.

Rapid population increase placed heavy demands on Sunderland's infrastructure. Vital public services were provided by various public bodies. The Municipal Authority, Poor Law Guardians and the School Board all erected buildings of note, while charitable organisations provided hospitals, almshouses and schools. A number of public buildings were erected by the Office of Works, the official government architects. Utilities like water and gas were provided by commercial bodies, and these imbued the town with new office buildings in a range of fashionable styles. Many of the developing town's requirements were for new building types, and architects had to innovate to fulfil these needs.

The expanding urban community needed churches and chapels in which to worship, and many of Sunderland's finest buildings lie within the field of ecclesiastical architecture. Architects were eager to design churches because their larger budgets allowed them to demonstrate the full extent of their talents. Holy Trinity is a well-preserved example of a Georgian church, boasting a Baroque reredos and much fine contemporary detail. Christ Church and St John's, Ashbrooke, represent the pinnacle of Sunderland's achievements in Gothic architecture: both are inspiring Victorian churches that reveal a thorough knowledge of medieval precedents. The latter was designed to put Sunderland Methodism on equal footing with the Established Church and is one of the best Nonconformist churches in the country. In St Andrew's, Roker, Sunderland possesses one of the best churches of the early twentieth century. Designed by the outstanding architect E.S. Prior, it houses contributions from leading members of the Arts and Crafts movement.

In common with William Morris and his followers, Prior aimed to unify art and craft and to free architecture from stylistic revivalism. These ideals are enshrined in a building widely known as the Cathedral of the Arts and Crafts movement. Although the church is a paean to the virtues of simple craftsmanship, with its innovative reinforced concrete structure and intellectual rigour it also anticipates many of the ideas central to the Modern Movement that dominated the architecture of the twentieth century. The valuing of form over applied decoration and the aversion to stylistic revivalism are characteristic, while the concern for truth to materials and structural honesty are the principal lessons that Modernists learned from their Arts and Crafts forebears.

In all this development Sunderland largely followed the patterns observed in comparable provincial towns, and thereby illuminates these patterns. Victorian architecture was characterised by contentious debates over which style was most appropriate for the industrial age and the host of modern building types to which it gave rise. These debates are reflected in the townscape of Sunderland. In the early nineteenth century Sunderland favoured the classical style for public buildings and even churches. By mid-century the Gothic Revival had established itself as the dominant ecclesiastical style, and its influence was felt throughout the town. Anglicans, Catholics and even Nonconformists produced churches and chapels that evoked the Middle Ages. As the Gothic Revival entered its High Victorian phase architects began to study French and Italian models, and a range of continental motifs began to appear in British architecture. These trends even left their imprint on secular buildings in Sunderland, including Frank Caws's Elephant Tea Rooms and the commercial designs of G.G. Hoskins. Renaissance styles became popular in the vigorous climate of commercial enterprise from about 1840 to 1880. Sunderland responded with Italianate banks and the French-inspired Museum and Library.

A century of steady development culminated in the Edwardian period, when Sunderland was crowned with a series of public and commercial buildings in the Baroque style, sometimes revealing the influence of continental Art Nouveau. Libraries, law courts, offices, theatres and public houses were designed in the vigorous Edwardian Baroque manner that was used throughout the country to express national and civic pride. Together, these buildings constitute the core of Sunderland's architectural legacy, and it is hoped they will be preserved for future generations.

In retrospect, the year 1907 represented the pinnacle of Sunderland's architectural achievement. St Andrew's Church was newly completed, along with the Empire Theatre and the River Wear Commissioners' impressive offices. Sunderland's prosperity, and by extension its architectural sophistication, began to decline soon after this highpoint, hastened by the cataclysm of the First World War.

There is always a dynamic of change within towns and cities. Since the Second World War Sunderland has experienced a period of renewal that has seen traditional industries in decline and their structures replaced. The central shopping area was completely remodelled and much housing was replaced by council estates. The turn of the twentieth and twenty-first centuries has witnessed a regeneration and renewal programme not unlike that which was experienced in the century before. In all this change it is important to cherish Sunderland's architectural heritage and to recall the contributions made by the architects and builders who created the city we know. Sunderland has a proud and distinctive identity, and this is embodied in the historic buildings that have survived within the changing townscape.

Bibliography

Addyman, J. and Haworth, V., *Robert Stephenson: Railway Engineer*, NERA and Robert Stephenson Trust, 2005

Anderson, A., *The Dream Palaces of Sunderland*, 1982

Anon., *A Rich Tapestry: Enon Baptist Church, Sunderland, 1834–1984*, 1984

Anon., *Centenary of St Joseph's Parish, Millfield, 1873–1973*, Sunderland, 1973

Anon., *Ewesley Road Methodist Church 75ᵀᴴ Anniversary*, 1979

Anon., *Freemasons' Hall, Queen St. East, Sunderland: 200ᵀᴴ Anniversary 1785–1985*

Anon., *In Memoriam. Robert Whitaker McAll*, 1898

Anon., *Old Sunderland*, 1977

Anon., *Parish of St Columba 1885–1935*, 1935

Anon., *St Mary's Jubilee 1835–1985*, 1985, n.p.

Anon., 'Sunderland Corporation Electricity Works, *The Electrician*, 5 September 1902, pp.779–84

Ayris, I. and Linsley, S.M., *A Guide to the Industrial Archaeology of Tyne and Wear*, 1994

Black, I.S., 'National Provincial Bank Buildings in North-East England in the later Nineteenth Century' in *Durham Archaeological Journal*, vol.17, 2003, pp.63–82

Black, J., *Presbyterianism in Sunderland and the North*, 1876

Blair, D.J., *The Spatial Dynamics of Commercial Activity in Central Sunderland*, unpublished MA dissertation, Durham University, 1977

Burgess, J., *Architects and Architecture of Northumberland and Durham*, 2008

Buscarlet, F.C. and Hunter, A., 'The Queen Alexandra Bridge over the River Wear, Sunderland', *Proceedings of the Institution of Civil Engineers*, 182, 1909–10, pp.59–93

Butler, D.M., *The Quaker Meeting Houses of Britain*, 1999

Chamberlain, A.G., *North East Architects and the Building Trade up to 1865*, 1986

Clark, K., *The Gothic Revival: An Essay in the History of Taste*, 1974

Collingwood, C.S., *Dr Cowan and the Grange School, Sunderland*, 1897

Colvin, H.M., *A Biographical Dictionary of English Architects, 1660–1840*, 1954

Colvin, H.M., *English Architectural History: A Guide to Sources*, 1967

Corder manuscripts, *Bishopwearmouth*

Corder manuscripts, *Family Pedigrees*

Corfe, T. (ed.), *Historical Atlas of County Durham*, 1993

Corfe, T., *A History of Sunderland*, 1973

Corfe, T., *Wearmouth Heritage*, 1975

Craggs, S.R., *Theses on North East England*, 1983

Crangle, L.P., *The Roman Catholic Community in Sunderland from the 16ᵀᴴ century*, 1969

Crosby, J.H., *Ignatius Bonomi of Durham, Architect*, 1987

Cumming, E. and Kaplan, W., *The Arts and Crafts Movement*, 1991

Cummings, C.L., 'Some Account of St George's Square and the People Connected Therewith', *Antiquities of Sunderland*, 7, 1906, pp.53–80

Cunningham, C., *Victorian and Edwardian Town Halls*, 1981

Curl, J.S., *Victorian Architecture*, 1990

Daunton, M.J., *House and Home in the Victorian City: Working Class Housing, 1850–1914*, 1983

Davey, P., *Arts and Crafts Architecture: The Search for Earthly Paradise*, 1980

Davison, P.J., *Brickworks of the North East*, 1986

Denby, F.W., 'A Memoir of the Late Joseph Oswald', *Archaeologia Aeliana*, series 4, vol.7, 1930, pp.179–83

Dennis, N., *People and Planning: the sociology of housing in Sunderland*, 1970

Dixon, R. and Muthesius, S., *Victorian Architecture*, 1978

Earl, J. and Sell, M., *The Theatres Trust Guide to British Theatres, 1750–1950*, 2000

Eden, F.M., *The State of the Poor*, 1797

Faughey, D., *Leisure in the Nineteenth Century with special reference to Sunderland*, unpublished Certificate of Education Dissertation, Sunderland Polytechnic, 1974

Faulkner, T.E., *Architects and Architecture of Newcastle upon Tyne and the North East*, 2000

Faulkner, T.E. and Greg, A., *John Dobson: Architect of the North East*, 2001

Faulkner, T.E. (ed), *Northumbrian Panorama*, 1996, pp.97–122

Faulkner, T.E., 'Robert James Johnson: Architect and Antiquary', *Durham University Journal*, 56 (1), January 1995, pp.3–11

Fawcett, B., *History of NER Architecture, vol. 3: Bell and Beyond*, NERA, 2005

Felstead, A., *et al.*, *RIBA Directory of British Architects 1834–1900*, 1993

Fordyce, W., *The History and Antiquities of the County Palatine of Durham*, 1857

Garbutt, G., *A Historical and Descriptive View of the Parishes of Monkwearmouth and Bishopwearmouth and the Port and Borough of Sunderland*, 1819

Garnham, T., 'Edward Prior: St Andrew's Church, Roker' in Dunlop, B. (ed.), *Arts and Crafts Masterpieces*, 1999, n.p.

Gettings, L., 'Benjamin Simpson, FRIBA: Part 1' in *Northern Architect*, new series, no.12, 1977, pp.28–31 and Part 2 in *Northern Architect*, new series, no.13, 1977, pp.33–8

Gibson, P., *History of Southwick*, 1986

Girouard, M., *Sweetness and Light: The 'Queen Anne' Movement, 1860–1900*, 1977

Girouard, M., *Victorian Pubs*, 1984

Goodhart-Rendel, H.S, 'Rogue Architects of the Victorian Era', *RIBA Journal* 56, 1953, pp.251–9

Gray, A.S., *Edwardian Architecture*, 1985

Greene, C.A.C., *Churches and their Building*, Sunderland, 1912

Green, F., *A Guide to the Historic Parks and Gardens of Tyne and Wear*, 1995

Greg, A., *The Tyneside Classical Tradition: classical architecture in the North East c.1700–1850*, 1980

Greg, A., *Victorian and Edwardian Architecture in the Northeast*, 1981

Harper, R.H., *Victorian Architectural Competitions: An Index to British and Irish Architectural Competitions in* The Builder *1843–1900*, 1983

Hawkes, D., 'St Andrew's, Roker' in *Architect's Journal*, vol.181, no.5, 1985

Hind, C., and McKinstry, J., *Architectural Images of the North 1700–1950*, 1998

Hutchins, R., *Sunderland Parish Church: A Short History*, 1982

Hutchinson, W., *The History and Antiquities of the County Palatine of Durham*, 1794

Hyslop, R., *200 Years 1739–1939*, 1939

Hyslop, R., 'The Fawcett Estate', *Antiquities of Sunderland*, XIX, 1929–32, pp.29–41

Inglis, S., *Engineering Archie: Archibald Leitch – football ground designer*, 2005

Jamieson, J., *Durham at the Opening of the Twentieth Century*, 1906

James, J.G., *The Iron Bridge at Sunderland*, unpublished paper, 1986

James, J.G., 'Thomas Wilson's Cast Iron Bridges 1800–1810' in *Transactions of the Newcomen*

Society, 50, 1978–79, pp.55–72

Johnson, M., 'Architects to a Diocese: Dunn and Hansom of Newcastle' in *Northern Catholic History*, no.49, 2008, pp.3–17

Johnson, M., *The Architecture of Dunn and Hansom of Newcastle upon Tyne*, unpublished MA Dissertation, University of Northumbria, 2003

Johnson, M., 'The Sunderland Cottage: "The favourite and typical dwelling of the skilled mechanic"' in *Vernacular Architecture*, vol.41, 2010, pp.59–74

Johnson, M., '"An Uncalculating Grasp of Beauty": St Andrew's Church, Roker, County Durham' in *Durham Archaeological Journal*, Nov. 2009

Johnson, R.J., 'St Peter's, Monkwearmouth', *Ecclesiologist*, vol.27, 1866, pp.361–64

Kamen, R.H., *British and Irish Architectural History*, 1981

Kitts, J.J., 'The Subscription Library' in *Antiquities of Sunderland*, IX, 1908

Longstaffe, E.A., *New Housing in Sunderland c.1860–1870*, unpublished BA Dissertation, Sunderland Polytechnic, 1982

Lowe, R.H., *Monkwearmouth Church in the 19TH Century*, Wearmouth Historical Pamphlet No. 6, n.d.

Mackintosh, I. and Sell, M. (eds), *Curtains!!!, or a New Life for Old Theatres*, 1982

Meadows, P. and Waterson, E., *Lost Houses of County Durham*, 1993

Milburn, G.E., *Church and Chapel*, 1988.

Milburn, G.E. and Miller, S.T. (eds), *Sunderland: River, Town and People: A history from the 1780s*, 1988

Milburn, G.E. (ed.), *St John's Ashbrooke: a church and its story 1888–1988*, 1988

Milburn, G.E., 'Tensions in Primitive Methodism in the Eighteen Seventies and the Origins of the Christian Lay Churches in the North East', *Proceedings of the Wesley Historical Society*, February 1976, pp.93–101 and 135–45

Mitchell, W.C., *History of Sunderland*, 1919

Monkwearmouth Local History Group, *More Monkwearmouth Memories*, 1990

Morris, M. and Gooch, L., *Down Your Aisles: the Diocese of Hexham and Newcastle 1850–2000*, 2000

Murray, J., 'Account of the removal of the Light-house at Sunderland', *Proceedings of the Institution of Civil Engineers*, 3, 1844, pp.342–55

Murray, J., 'On the Progressive Construction of the Sunderland Docks', *Proceedings of the Institution of Civil Engineers*, 15, 1855–56, pp.418–55

Orbach, J., *Blue Guide: Victorian Architecture in Britain*, 1987

Patterson, G., 'Harrison's Buildings – Sunderland's First Council Housing', *Sunderland's History*, 3, 1985, pp.5–34

Pearson, L.F., 'The Architecture of Entertainment Run Riot: William Hope of Newcastle, 1862–1907', *Northern History*, 27, 1991, pp.184–97

Pearson, L.F., *Index of North Eastern Architects 1860–1914*, 1991

Pearson, L.F., *The Northumbrian Pub: An Architectural History*, 1989

Pevsner, N. and Williamson, E., *The Buildings of England: County Durham*, 1983

Pevsner, N. and Williamson, E., *The Buildings of England: County Durham*, 2002

Phillips, M., *A History of Banks, Bankers and Banking in Northumberland, Durham and North Yorkshire*, 1894

Pickersgill, A., *Sunderland in Times Past*, 1981

Potts, G.R., *A Biographical Dictionary of Sunderland Architects 1800–1914*, 2007, typescript in Sunderland Local Studies Library

Potts, G.R., 'Frank Caws: Sunderland Architect' in *Sunderland's History*, 1998

Potts, G.R., 'Methodist Chapels and the Gothic Revival', *Proceedings of the Wesley Historical Society*, May 1991

Potts, T., *Sunderland: A History of the Town, Port and Commerce*, 1892

Prior, E.S., 'Texture as a quality of art and a condition for architecture' in *Transactions of the National Association for the Advancement of Art and its Application to Industry – Edinburgh Meeting*, 1890

Prior, E.S., 'Church building as it is and as it might be' in *Architectural Review*, 4, 1898, pp.106–08; 154–58

Prior, E.S., *A History of Gothic Art in England*, 1900

Prior, E.S., *Eight Chapters on English Medieval Art*, 1922

Pritchett, H.D., *The Bridges of the County of Durham*, 1931

Rennison, R., *Civil Engineering Heritage: Northern England*, 1996

Richardson, M.A., *The Local Historian's Table Book*, 1844

Richardson, R. and Thorne, R., *The Builder Illustrations Index 1843–1883*, 1994

Ritson, J., 'Primitive Methodism in Sunderland', *Primitive Methodist Magazine*, 67, 1886, pp.19–23 and 85–87

Robinson, J., 'Some Historic Houses in Sunderland, illustrated with plans and photographs' in *Antiquities of Sunderland*, IV, 1903

Robinson, W., *The Story of the Royal Infirmary, Sunderland*, 1934

Rounthwaite, R.S., 'Sunderland Hospital Accommodation', *Proceedings of the Institution of Municipal and County Engineers*, 15, 23 March 1889, pp.28–33

Royal Commission of Historic Monuments, *An Architectural Survey of Urban Development Corporation areas: Tyne and Wear*, 1990

Ruscoe, J.E., *The Churches of the Diocese of Durham: a pictorial guide*, 1994

Ruskin, J., *The Seven Lamps of Architecture*, 1849

Ryder, R., 'Council house building in County Durham, 1900–1939: the local implementation of national policy' in Daunton, M.J. (ed.), *Councillors and Tenants: Local Authority Housing in English Cities, 1919–1939*, 1984, pp.40–100

Scarff, W., *Durham in the Twentieth Century*, 1906.

Service, A., *Edwardian Architecture: A Handbook to Building Design in Britain, 1890–1914*, 1977

Service, A., (ed.) *Edwardian Architecture and its Origins*, 1975

Sinclair, N.T., *The River Wear*, 1984

Staddon, S.A., *The Tramways of Sunderland*, 1964

Stell, C., *An Inventory of Nonconformist Chapels and Meeting Houses in the North of England*, 1994

Stevenson, J.J., *House Architecture*, 1880

Summers, J.W., *History and Antiquities of Sunderland, Bishopwearmouth and Monkwearmouth*, 1858

Surtees, R., *The History and Antiquities of the County Palatine of Durham*, 1816–40 (three vols)

Sykes, J., *Local Records*, 1866

Tasker, D.H., *Housing and Public Health in Victorian Sunderland c.1840–1905*, unpublished BA dissertation, Hull University, 1986

Usherwood, P., *et al.*, *Public Sculpture of North East England*, 2000

Walker, A., 'The Church of St Andrew', *Northern Architect*, 17, January 1979, pp.19–24

Watts Moses, E., *To Ashbrooke and Beyond: The History of Sunderland Cricket and Rugby Football Club, 1808–1963*, 1963

Wickstead, J., *C. Hodgson Fowler; Durham Architect and his Churches*, DCLHS, 2001

Weiner, D., *Architecture and Social Reform*, 1994.

Wood, J., *Town Atlas of Northumberland and Durham, 1820–7*, 1991.

Wood, P.A., *Activities of the Sunderland Poor Law Union, 1834–1930*, unpublished M.Litt dissertation, Newcastle University, 1975

Woodward, G., 'Trubshaw, Hartley and Harrison: early nineteenth century engineers and architects', *Transactions of the Newcomen Society*, 2001

Glossary of Architectural Terms

Aedicule – Architectural surround to a door or window, usually consisting of two columns or pilasters supporting a pediment. The term literally means 'little building'.

Aisle – Space running longitudinally down the nave of a church on either side.

Alabaster – Building material composed of sulphate of lime or gypsum. It is usually white and translucent, but is sometimes red or yellow.

Ambulatory – Aisle running around the apse at the ritual east end of a church.

Anthemion – Design consisting of a number of radiating petals, developed by the Ancient Greeks.

Apse – Semicircular or polygonal space at the end of a church or chapel, housing the chancel.

Arcade – Series of arches supported by piers or columns.

Architrave – Lowest member of a classical entablature. Essentially an elaborate lintel, it occurs over doors or windows.

Ashlar – Stone that has been worked to produce a flat surface, straight edges and a regular shape. It is more expensive than rough stone, and is often used to give definition to the edges or details of a building.

Atrium – Originally the inner court of a Roman house. Frequently used in multi-storey buildings to illuminate the interior via a skylight.

Baluster – One of a series of short posts or pillars that support a rail, thus forming a balustrade.

Balustrade – Series of balusters supporting a handrail.

Baroque – Style of architecture, painting and sculpture that originated in Rome c.1600. Baroque architecture is characterised by dramatic massing, often with concave and convex façades. It was current in Britain c.1680–1720, and was revived in the Edwardian era c.1901–14.

Basilica – Roman public hall taking the form of an aisled building with a clerestory.

Bay – Internal compartment of a building, divided from each other by columns or pilasters. Bays can also be defined by fenestration (windows).

Bay Window – Window with a straight front and angled sides projecting from the face of a building.

Bow Window – Curved window projecting from the face of a building.

Belfry – The stage in a tower that houses bells.

Bell Cote – Gable or turret used for hanging bells when there is no belfry.

Belvedere – Literally 'fair view', a structure sited to take advantage of such a view.

Bond – The way in which bricks are laid. In English Bond bricks are laid so that alternate courses are composed entirely of headers or stretchers. In Flemish Bond headers and stretchers alternate in each course.

Blind Arch – Arch that is applied to a wall for decorative purposes, without an opening inside the arch.

Bracket – Member made of wood, stone, or metal that overhangs a wall to support a weight.

Broach Spire – Octagonal spire rising from a square tower, the transition between structures effected by pyramidal forms called broaches.

Buttress – Vertical member attached to a wall to provide stability, often used to define the bays.

Canted – Angled at the sides.

Capital – Top part of a column, often sculpted in different decorative forms known as the Classical Orders.

Cartouche – Decorative panel of stone or plaster.

Chamfer – Surface made by cutting across the square edge of a block of stone, piece of wood etc., at an angle of 45 degrees.

Chancel – Space at the ritual east end of a church housing the altar and set apart for the use of the officiating clergy.

Classicism – Style of architecture devised by the Ancient Greeks and Romans.

Clerestory – Upper storey of a church, which rises above the aisle roofs, containing windows. Its function is to illuminate the church.

Coffering – Decorative treatment of ceilings, vaults or arches in which the surface is lined with square or polygonal sunken panels (coffers).

Colonnade – Series of columns supporting an entablature.

Column – Upright structural member with a round cross section. It usually has a base, shaft and capital.

Console – Bracket with a curved outline.

Corbel – Projecting block that supports a structure such as a gallery or roof beam. Often carved into a decorative form.

Cornice – Highest member of a classical entablature, a flat-topped ledge with a moulded underside. It also occurs as a decorative moulding between a wall and ceiling.

Course – Continuous layer of brick or stone making up the wall of a building.

Crenellation – Decorative treatment consisting of square indentations like those in the battlements of a castle.

Crocket – Decorative element common in Gothic architecture in the form of curled leaves.

Crossing – In a cruciform church, the space formed by the junction of the nave and the transepts.

Cupola – Small domed turret crowning a roof.

Dais – Raised platform for dignified occupancy. Historically the dais was part of the floor at the end of a medieval hall, raised a step above the rest of the room.

Dentils – Series of small square blocks used in classical cornices.

Diocletian window – Large semicircular window characteristic of the enormous public baths of Ancient Rome.

Dormer – Window rising vertically from the incline of a roof.

Dressed Stone – Blocks of stone that have been worked to produce a smooth face.

Dripmould – Projection from a cornice or sill designed to protect the area below from rainwater.

Eaves – The parts of a sloping roof that overhang.

Elevation – One of the external faces of a building.

Encaustic tiles – Ceramic tiles in which the pattern on the surface is the product of different colours of clay rather than of a surface glaze.

Entablature – In classical architecture, the horizontal member carried by a wall or columns. It is composed of three main elements: architrave, frieze and cornice.

Escutcheon – Shield-shaped emblem, displaying a coat of arms.

Façade – External face of a building, usually the main one.

Faïence – Glazed clay tile or block.

Fascia – Plain horizontal band in an architrave. Often used on shopfronts.

Fenestration – The arrangement of windows in a façade.

Festoon – String or garland of leaves or flowers, suspended in a loop between two points.

Finial – Small sculpted ornament at the top of a gable or pinnacle.

Fleche – Pointed spike or finial, common on church roofs.

Flemish Gable – Gable with tiered and curved sides as evolved in the Low Countries. Also known as a Dutch gable.

Fleur-de-lys – Stylised lily design, which served as a symbol for the French monarchy.

Fluting – Decorative treatment of columns and pilasters in which vertical channels are cut into the surface.

Foliated – Carved with leaf forms.

Frieze – Middle member of a classical entablature, between the architrave and the cornice. The term can also refer to a decorative horizontal band along the upper part of an interior wall.

Gallery – Raised section of seating in a church.

Gargoyle – Grotesque carving in the form of a human, animal or mythical beast, at the end of a water spout.

Georgian – The period during the reign of the four Georges (1714–1830). In architecture it saw the rise of Palladianism, Neoclassicism, Rococo, Chinoiserie and Gothic.

Gothic – Style of architecture that was prevalent in Western Europe from about 1200 until 1550. In England, Gothic is normally divided into three succeeding phases – Early English, Decorated and Perpendicular. Characteristic features include pointed arches, flying buttresses and windows with ornate tracery.

Gothick – Eighteenth-century style only vaguely based on archaeologically correct Gothic, and more connected with a taste for the grotesque.

Grotesque – Ornament used principally in Gothic architecture consisting of representations of mythical beasts and grotesque figures.

Half-timbering – Method of construction in which the walls are built of timber framework and the spaces are filled with plaster or brickwork.

Hammer Beam – Short horizontal beam, usually made of wood, extending from the top of a masonry wall outward towards the centre of the enclosed space, but not completely traversing it. The projecting end is usually connected to the roof with a diagonal brace.

Hipped Roof – A roof sloping at the ends as well as the sides.

Hood-mould – Arched covering used to throw off rainwater.

Inglenook – Small recess that adjoins a fireplace.

Keystone – Wedge-shaped stone placed at the top of an arch to provide downward thrust.

Lancet – In Gothic architecture, a long, narrow window with a pointed head. It is particularly characteristic of the Early English phase of Gothic architecture.

Lantern – Windowed turret surmounting a roof or dome.

Lectern – Reading stand in a church.

Light – Opening between the mullions of a window.

Linenfold – Style of relief carving used to decorate wood panelling, resembling folded linen. Originally from Flanders, the style became widespread across Northern Europe in the fourteenth to sixteenth centuries.

Loggia – Colonnaded gallery, usually on the exterior of a building.

Lozenge – Diamond shape.

Lucarne – Small gabled opening in a roof or spire.

Manse – House inhabited by a minister, usually of the Presbyterian or Methodist denominations.

Minaret – A feature of Islamic mosques, generally a tall spire with an onion-shaped or conical crown, used to issue the call to prayer.

Modillions – Curved brackets along the underside of a cornice.

Mullion – Vertical post dividing a window into lights.

Narthex – Porch or vestibule of a church, placed before the nave.

Nave – The central space within a church, extending from the narthex to the chancel and flanked by aisles.

Niche – Shallow recess in a wall, usually housing a statue or similar ornament.

Obelisk – Four-sided shaft of stone, tapering to a pyramidal top.

Oeil de bœuf – Literally bullseye, a small oval or circular window.

Ogee – a double curve, bending first one way then the other. Used in certain arches or roofs.

Orders – The formalised versions of the post-and-lintel system in classical architecture. The main orders are Doric, Ionic, and Corinthian. They are Greek in origin but occur in Roman versions.

Oriel – Window that projects from an upper storey of a building.

Overlight – Glazed opening over a door or window.

Palladian – Architecture following the principles of the Italian Renaissance architect Andrea Palladio (1508–80).

Pagoda – General term for a tiered tower with multiple eaves common in India, China, Japan and other parts of Asia.

Pantile – Roofing tile with an S-shaped cross-section.

Parapet – Low wall used to conceal a roof.

Patera – Originally a broad, shallow dish used for drinking in a ritual context such as a libation. Also used as an architectural detail.

Pavilion – Free-standing structure sited a short distance from a main residence. The term can also be applied to the outer wings of a building if they are emphasised in some way.

Pedestal – Architectural support for a statue or other ornamental form.

Pediment – In classical and Renaissance architecture, a low-pitched gable occurring above a portico, door or window. It is usually triangular or segmental. In a broken pediment, a portion of the sloping sides is left open. In an open pediment a portion of the base is left open.

Perpendicular – Style of English Gothic architecture dating from the fourteenth and fifteenth centuries, characterised by a strong vertical emphasis.

Piano Nobile – Principal floor of a classical building, usually the first floor, distinguished from the other floors by richer ornamentation.

Piazza – City square or pedestrian space in front of a significant building.

Pier – Any strong, structural support.

Pilaster – Flat, square-faced column projecting from a wall.

Pinnacle – Pointed termination of a spire or buttress, etc.

Plinth – Projecting base of a wall.

Portico – Porch leading to the entrance of a building, usually consisting of a pediment supported by columns.

Pulpit – Raised platform in a church from which sermons are delivered.

Pulvinated Frieze – In classical and Renaissance architecture, a convex frieze that resembles a pillow or cushion in profile.

Quadrangle – Inner courtyard within a large building.

Quatrefoil – Ornamental form consisting of four foils or lobes.

Quoins – Dressed stones at the angles of a building.

Reredos – Ornamental screen behind an altar.

Reveal – The part of the side of a window or door that is between the outer surface of a wall and the window or door frame.

Rock-faced – Descriptive term for stonework that is squared off along the edges, but in which the face is left as it was split at the quarry.

Romanesque – Style of architecture that flourished in Western Europe between 1050 and 1200. The style derives its name from the fact that it drew much of its influence from Roman architecture. In England it is also called the Norman style. Characteristic features include round arches and massive pillars.

Roundel – a curved form, especially a semicircular panel, window or recess.

Rustication – Exaggerated treatment of masonry to give an effect of strength. The joints are usually recessed by V-section chamfering.

Sacristy – In a church, a strong room usually attached to the north side of the chancel where vestments and the utensils belonging to the altars are placed.

Sash Window – Window with sliding glazed frames, imported to England from Holland in the late seventeenth century.

Segmental – Term applied to a curved element resembling a section of a circle.

Snecked – Irregular masonry, with courses broken by smaller stones (snecks).

Soffit – The exposed undersurface of any overhead component of a building such as an arch.

Spandrel – The space between an arch and its containing rectangle, or between adjacent arches.

Spire – Tapering structure that rises from a tower or roof.

Stanchion – Upright structural member of iron or steel, etc.

Stiff-leaf – Foliage ornament typical of the Early English style.

String Course – Continuous horizontal band in the surface of a wall.

Stucco – Lime-based render applied to the exterior of a building.

Swag – Decorative carving representing a suspended cloth or curtain.

Swan-necked pediment – Pediment in which the cornice is in the form of two S-shaped brackets.

Terracotta – Literally 'baked earth'. Moulded and fired clay ornament.

Tracery – Delicate stonework that supports the glass in a Gothic window.

Transept – Part of a church that runs perpendicular to the nave, forming a cruciform floor plan.

Triptych – Work of art divided into three carved panels which are hinged together and folded.

Triumphal arch – In Roman architecture, a monumental structure pierced by at least one arched passageway and erected to honour an important person or to commemorate a significant event.

Tudor – Architectural style flourishing during the Tudor period (1485–1603). The four-centred or Tudor arch is characteristic.

Turret – Small tower, usually round or polygonal in plan.

Tympanum – The space within a pediment, often bearing ornamentation.

Undercroft – Subterranean room under a church, used as a chapel or for any sacred purpose.

Vault – Roof or ceiling constructed of masonry on the arch principle. A barrel vault is semi-cylindrical in cross section.

Venetian window – Window composed of three lights, the central light arched and the two flanking lights with flat heads.

Vernacular – Based on local and traditional construction methods, materials and styles.

Vestry – The room in a church where the clergy stored their vestments.

Viaduct – Bridge composed of several small spans. The term is derived from the Latin *via* for road and *ducere* to lead something.

Voussoir – Wedge-shaped stone used in constructing an arch.

Wainscoting – Panelling applied to the lower part of an interior wall, below the dado rail and above the skirting board.

Endnotes

1   G. Cookson, *Sunderland: Building a City*, 2010, p.108.

2   A coal-fitter was an individual who acted as a middle man between the colliery owner and the end user of the coal.

3   See Census for 1801 and 1901. However, population figures were affected by boundary changes. During the period under study, Sunderland Borough boundaries were extended in 1867 and 1895. G.E. Milburn and S.T. Miller, *Sunderland: River, Town and People*, 1988, p.222 gives fuller figures.

4   R. Hutchins, *Sunderland Parish Church: a short history*, n.d, p.6.

5   H.M. Colvin, *A Biographical Dictionary of British Architects 1600–1840*, 1995, pp.354–55.

6   The pews were designed by Wood and Oakley. See Tyne and Wear Archive Service, DT.WO/4/156. The architects were instructed to use oak from the original box pews as far as possible.

7   Galleries were built along the north and south walls in 1842. These were removed in 1935 and the west gallery was refashioned.

8   J. Sykes, *Local Records*, 1866, p248, p.268.

9   G. Cookson, op. cit., 2010, p.79.

10   H.M. Colvin, op. cit., 1995, pp.354–55.

11   G. Cookson, op. cit., 2010, p.72.

12   G. Cookson, op. cit., 2010, p.72.

13   Corder Manuscripts, vol.29 for Thornhill; T. Corfe (ed.), *The Buildings of Sunderland 1814–1914*, 1983, p.14. Corder Manuscripts, Family Pedigrees, 4, pp.343–45.

14   F.M. Eden, *The State of the Poor*, 1797, pp.185–87.

15   R. Surtees, *History and Antiquities of the County of Durham: Sunderland and District Section*, 1908, p.14.

16   G. Cookson, op. cit., 2010, p.23.

17   J.G. James, 'The Old Cast Iron Bridge', G.E. Milburn and S.T. Miller (eds), *Sunderland: River, Town and People*, 1988, pp.8–9; J.G. James, 'Thomas Wilson's Cast Iron Bridges 1800–1810', *Transactions of the Newcomen Society*, 50, 1978–79, pp.55–72; J.G. James, *The Iron Bridge at Sunderland*, unpublished paper, 1986.

18   Durham County Record Office, Q/D/P/223; *Illustrated London News*, 19 Feb 1859, p186. J. Addyman and V. Haworth, *Robert Stephenson: Railway Engineer*, NERA and Robert Stephenson Trust, 2005, p144.

19   Originally these were windows, but they were later blocked up. Anon., *Freemasons' Hall, Queen St. East, Sunderland: 200ᵀᴴ Anniversary 1785–1985*; N. Pevsner and E. Williamson, *Buildings of England: County Durham*, 1983, p.455.

20   G. Garbutt, *A Historical and Descriptive View of the Parishes of Monkwearmouth and Bishopwearmouth and the Port and Borough of Sunderland*, 1819, p.327; W. Fordyce, *Durham II*, 1857, p.474.

21   G. Garbutt, op. cit., p.327.

22   *Sunderland Herald*, 14 October 1837, p.2 and 25 November 1837, p.3.

23   *Sunderland Herald*, 25 January 1851.

24   N. Pevsner and E. Williamson, op. cit., 1983, p.457; *Sunderland Year Book*, 1904, pp.23–25.

25   W. Fordyce, *Durham II*, 1857, pp.467–68; *Sunderland Herald*, 5 May 1854, p.4; P.A. Wood, *Activities of the Sunderland Poor Law Union 1834–1930*, unpublished M.Litt dissertation, Newcastle University, 1975.

26   *Building News*, 65, 8 December 1893, p.73; *Builder* 83, 27 September 1902, p.279.

27   *Building News*, 14 March 1890, p.397.

28   W. Robinson, *The Story of the Royal Infirmary, Sunderland*, 1934, p.46.

29   *Building News*, 15, 3 January 1868, p.16; Sunderland Museum, Print C12805.

30   *Building News*, 64, 8 December 1893, p.469.

31   *Sunderland Daily Echo*, 15 April 1895, p.3.

32   *Building News*, 26 September 1890, p.453.

33   R.S. Rounthwaite, 'Sunderland Hospital Accommodation', *Proceedings of the Institution of Municipal and County Engineers*, 15, 23 March 1889, pp.28–33; *Sunderland Daily Echo*, 15 January 1907, p.3.

34   *Building News*, 92, 22 March 1907, pp.417–18; *Sunderland Daily Echo*, 29 and 30 May 1912.

35   *Northern Times*, 10 April 1840, p.1; *Sunderland Herald*, 1 January 1841, p.5.

36   *Sunderland Herald*, 8 May 1863, p.5; *Building News*, 11, 5 February 1864, p.105.

37   *Building News*, 4, 26 November 1858, p.1184; *Sunderland Herald*, 14 December 1860, p.7.

38   *Sunderland Herald*, 16 May 1856, p.5.

39   *Sunderland Times*, 31 October 1868, p.5.

40   *Sunderland Daily Echo*, 19 September 1882, pp.2–3.

41   *Builder*, 88, 20 May 1905, p.548; *Sunderland Daily Echo*, 15 May 1905, p.6.

42   *Sunderland Daily Echo*, 1 February 1877, p.3 and 15 February 1877, p.4.

43   *Oxford Dictionary of National Biography Online*, 2006; R. Rennison, *Civil Engineering Heritage: Northern England*, 1996, p.69.

44   *Sunderland Daily Echo*, 8 August 1905, p.5.

45   Information from N.T. Sinclair; *Sunderland Times*, 18 December 1869, p.4.

46   W. Fordyce, *Durham II*, 1857, p.430; information from N.T. Sinclair.

47   W. Fordyce, *Durham II*, 1857, p.430; *Sunderland Herald*, 25 January 1856, p.1.

48   *Sunderland Herald*, 7 May 1858, p.7.

49   *Builder*, 13, 1855, p.345.

50   *Sunderland Herald*, 11 April 1848, p.5; 18 January 1850, p.7; 11 April 1851, p.5 and 12 November 1852, p.8.

51   W. Fordyce, *Durham II*, 1857, p.422; *Sunderland Herald*, 15 January 1858, p.8.

52   T. Oliver Jr, *Baths and Wash-houses: their intention, construction and cost. Illustrated with plans, elevations, sections*, 1852.

53   *Sunderland Daily Echo*, 10 July 1890, p.4; *Building News*, 90, 1 June 1906, p.790.

54   *Sunderland Herald*, 22 October 1852, p.4; 26 November 1852, p.5; 4 January 1856, p.8; 20 June 1856, p.4; D. Faughey, *Leisure in the Nineteenth Century with special reference to Sunderland*, unpublished Cert Ed Dissertation, Sunderland Polytechnic, 1974, pp.57–68.

55   *Sunderland Herald*, 13 July 1866, p.7 and 26 July 1867, p.8; handbill and Donkin's design in Newcastle City Library, Miscellaneous Sunderland Items; *Sunderland Times*, 11 July 1866, pp.2–4.

56   *Sunderland Daily Echo*, 23 June 1880, p.2 and 24 June 1880, p.3.

57   *Building News*, 3 October 1890, p.489.

58   *Building News*, 59, 3 October 1890, p.489; *Sunderland Daily Echo*, 9 January 1907, p.3.

59   *Sunderland Daily Echo*, 30 December 1907, p.3; 5 August 1909, p.3; *Sunderland Year Book*, 1906, p.71 and plan.

60   *Kelly's Directory*, 1894, p.361; *Sunderland Daily Echo*, 5 August 1903, p.3 and 6 November 1906, p.3.

61   This story has been told more fully in G.R. Potts, 'Sunderland Town Hall', G.E. Milburn and S.T. Miller, op. cit., 1988, pp.164–65 and plates; G.R. Potts, 'Frank Caws: Sunderland Architect, *Sunderland's History*, 10, 2003, pp.7–22.

62   Town Hall Committee Minutes, TWAS, SDP/A15/1/1; *Sunderland Herald*, 6 November 1890, pp.2–3.

63   *Building News*, 19 December 1890, p.873 and plate.

64   *British Architect*, 4 March 1904, p.168 and plate.

65   W. Fordyce, *Durham II*, 1857, p.477; *Sunderland Daily Echo*, 25 August 1900, p.3.

66   For a discussion of the building's significance see S. Kane, 'When Paris Meets Teesdale: the Bowes Museum, Barnard Castle' in T.E. Faulkner, *Northumbrian Panorama: Studies in the History and Culture of North East England*, 1996, pp.163–94.

67   *Building News*, 32, 23 March 1877, p.289; L. Jessup and N.T. Sinclair, *Sunderland Museum*, 1996.

68   *Sunderland Daily Echo*, 7 May 1906, p.3; 26 February 1907, p.4; 26 January 1909, p.4; 29 June 1909, p.3.

69   When the results of the competitions were announced it was found that Davidson and Cratney of Newcastle and Sunderland had won first and second positions in both the Monkwearmouth and Hendon competitions. This prompted the committee to re-examine the plans to make sure that the conditions of both competitions had been fulfilled. *Builder*, 20 April 1907, p.481.

70   *Builder*, 83, 13 September 1902, pp.227–28.

71   C.S. Collingwood, *Dr Cowan and the Grange School, Sunderland*, 1897.

72   *Sunderland Daily Echo*, 7 February 1888, p.3 and 22 July 1891, p.3.

73   J. Sykes, *Local Records II*, 1866, p.42; Sunderland Museum, Plan; P. Gibson, *Southwick*, 1986, p.5 and plate.

74   *Sunderland Herald*, 21 November 1856, p.1. *Newcastle Courant*, 14 July 1854; *Sunderland Herald*, 21 November 1866, p.7.

75   *Sunderland Herald*, 15 April 1859, p.5.

76   *Building News*, 7, 20 September 1861, p.771; *Sunderland Daily Echo*, 24 February 1876, p.3. William Forster was Londonderry Company architect *c.* 1865–97.

77   The designs for the first thirty London Board Schools were selected by limited competition. After Robson's appointment, he and his staff of fifteen designed every school. His salary was soon increased to £1,000. See D. Weiner, *Architecture and Social Reform*, 1994, p.64.

78   *Builder*, 35, 17 March 1877, p.275.

79   *Building News*, 25, 9 May 1873, pp.525–26; *Sunderland Times*, 9 January 1874, p.6.

80   G.R. Potts, *A Biographical Dictionary of Sunderland Architects 1800–1914*, 2007, typescript in Sunderland Local Studies Library.

81   *Sunderland Daily Echo*, 27 February 1884, p.2.

82   *Sunderland Daily Echo*, 1 August 1895, p.3.

83   *Sunderland Daily Echo*, 28 April 1890, p.3.

84   *Sunderland Daily Echo*, 12 August 1907, p.4; G.R. Potts, op. cit., 2007.

85   *Building News*, 73, 2 July 1897, p.11 and plate; *Sunderland Daily Echo*, 27 September 1899, p.3.

86   G.E. Milburn and S.T. Miller, *Sunderland: River, Town and People*, p.152.

87   G.E. Milburn, 'Religion in Sunderland in 1851', *Durham County Local History Society Bulletin*, 18, April 1975, pp.2–28.

88   J.M. Robinson, *The Wyatts: an architectural dynasty*, 1979.

89   W. Fordyce, *Durham II*, 1857, p.436.

90   M.A. Richardson, *The Local Historian's Table Book, V*, 1844, pp.219–20 and 338–9; *Sunderland and Durham County Herald*, 17 December 1841.

91   W. Fordyce, *Durham II*, 1857, p.443.

92   W. Fordyce, *Durham II*, 1857, p.439.

93   DCRO, EP/Biw866.

94   H.M. Colvin, op. cit., 1995, p.532; W. Fordyce, *Durham II*, 1857, p.443.

95   Further alterations took place in 1877. A vestry and cloister-like arcade were added to the north-east corner of the church and a residence for the verger was built alongside. In the church itself the font was reduced in height and re-sited. A new pulpit of Bath stone was substituted for the original and Minton's encaustic floor-tiles were laid in the chancel. The additions were orchestrated by the architect James Lindsay. See *Sunderland Daily Echo*, 1 September 1877, p.2.

96   This window has been reassembled in St Michael's Church, Bishopwearmouth.

97   H.G. Bowling, 'A Century at Christ Church', *Christ Church 1864–1964*, 1964. The spire of the church became unsafe and the building was sold for a Sikh temple (currently in the church hall), so the Christian furnishings have been removed.

98   D. Goldie, *The Story of a Mother Church, 1214–1964*, 1964, p.6.

99   *Sunderland Times*, 21 February 1871, p.2 and 29 November 1872, p.8.

100 *Sunderland Times*, 3 September 1870, p.8; Whellan, *Directory*, 1894, pp.846–47.

101 *Architect*, 1, 16 January 1869, p.41; *Sunderland Times*, 30 April 1872 and 4 May 1872; H. Ritson, *The 'Ritual' of St Mark's*, 1873.

102 G.E. Milburn, *Church and Chapel*, 1988, p.47.

103 *Sunderland Times*, 21 May 1872; *British Architect*, 2, 11 September 1874, p.173; C.H.G. Hopkins, *Pallion 1874–1954: Church and People in a Shipyard Parish*, 1954.

104 *British Architect*, 2, 13 November 1874, p.312.

105 *Sunderland Times*, 6 August 1870, p.8.

106 *Builder*, 28, 20 August 1870, p.673.

107 *British Architect*, 2, 25 September 1874, p.205.

108 J. Wickstead, *C Hodgson Fowler; Durham Architect and his Churches*, Durham County Local History Society, 2001.

109 *Sunderland Daily Echo*, 22 June 1880, p.4.

110 *Building News*, 57, 5 July 1889, p.31; 58, 21 February 1890, pp.80–81; 270 and plate.

111 *Building News*, 21 February 1890, p.270.

112 *Sunderland Daily Echo*, 16 June 1888, p.4; 19 February 1890, p.2; Anon., *Parish of St Columba 1885–1935*, 1935.

113 G.E. Milburn, *Church and Chapel*, 1988, p.48.

114 T.E. Faulkner, 'Robert James Johnson: Architect and Antiquary', *Durham University Journal*, 56 (1), January 1995, pp.3–11.

115 *Sunderland Herald*, 15 November 1867, p.5 and 13 December 1867, p.7; *Architect*, 13, 29 May 1875, p.325; R.H. Lowe, *Monkwearmouth Church in the 19ᵀᴴ Century*, Wearmouth Historical Pamphlet No. 6, n.d.

116 *Sunderland Herald*, 10 August 1866, p.5.

117 *Sunderland Daily Echo*, 29 January 1879, p.2.

118 *William Searle Hicks, Architect: In Memoriam*, Newcastle, 1903.

119 *Building News*, 55, 19 October 1888, p.525; 23 November 1888, p.69 and plan.

120 Full details at www.artefacts.co.za.

121 *Sunderland Daily Echo*, 18 May 1892, p.3; *Building News*, 59, 7 November 1890, p.342 and plate.

122 *Sunderland Daily Echo*, 25 October 1909, p.6 and 27 June 1910, p.6.

123 *Building News*, 9, 30 September 1910, p.471; *Sunderland Daily Echo*, 28 September 1911, p.6.

124 The architect and critic H.S. Goodhart–Rendel used this memorable phrase to describe a number of wilful architects of the nineteenth century, including William Butterfield, E.B. Lamb and E.S. Prior. See H.S. Goodhart-Rendel, 'Rogue Architects of the Victorian Era', *RIBA Journal*, 56, 1953, pp.251–59.

125 Prior quoted in D. Hawkes, 'St Andrew's, Roker' in *Architect's Journal*, 181 (5), 1985, p.27.

126 Ibid., p.15.

127 *Builder*, 93, 1907, pp.385–6; *Sunderland Daily Echo*, 12 June 1906, p.3; 13 June 1906, p.3 and sketch; 18 July 1907, p.3; A. Walker, 'The Church of St Andrew', *Northern Architect*, 17, January 1979, pp.19–24; T. Garnham, 'Edward Prior: St Andrew's Church, Roker' in B. Dunlop (ed.), *Arts and Crafts Masterpieces*, 1999, n.p.

128 *Building News*, 98, 10 June 1910, pp.794–5 with plan and plate; C.A. Clayton Greene, *Churches and their Building*, Sunderland, 1912.

129 *St Mary's Jubilee 1835–1985*, 1985, n.p.

130 J.H. Crosby, *Ignatius Bonomi of Durham: Architect*, Durham, 1987.

131 *Sunderland Herald*, 27 September 1834, p.2; W. Fordyce, *Durham II*, 1857, p.444; *St Mary's Jubilee*, Chapter 1.

132 *Sunderland Herald*, 23 March 1860, p.1.

133 M.A. Johnson, *The Architecture of Dunn and Hansom of Newcastle upon Tyne*, unpublished MA Dissertation, University of Northumbria, 2003; *Sunderland Daily Echo*, 28 July 1888, p.4 and 15 July 1889.

134 *Building News*, 2 February 1883, p.126.

135 *Sunderland Daily Echo*, 25 September 1902, p.3.

136 *Sunderland Times*, 12 July 1872, p.8 and 16 September 1873, p.2.

137 *Sunderland Daily Echo*, 4 July 1906, p.3; *Centenary of St Joseph's Parish, Millfield, 1873–1973*, Sunderland, 1973; G.R. Potts, *A Biographical Dictionary of Sunderland Architects 1800–1914*, 2007, typescript in Sunderland Local Studies Library.

138 *Sunderland Daily Echo*, 15 April 1909, p.4.

139 *Sunderland Daily Echo*, 23 February 1915, p.6.

140 *St Mary's Jubilee*, Education Chapter; *Sunderland Daily Echo*, 7 August 1917, p.6; *Sunderland Daily Echo*, 7 August 1900, p.3; 31 October 1907, p.3.

141 Information from G.E. Milburn; *Sunderland Year Book*, 1905, illustration, p.136.

142 Religious Census, 1851; *Whellan's Directory*, 1856, p.666.

143 Anon., *A Rich Tapestry: Enon Baptist Church, Sunderland, 1834–1984*, 1984.

144 T. Corfe (ed.), op. cit., 1983, p.25.

145 *Primitive Methodist Magazine*, 39, 1858, pp.682–3; J. Ritson, 'Primitive Methodism in Sunderland', *Primitive Methodist Magazine*, 67, 1886, pp.19–23 and 85–87

146 G. Garbutt, op. cit., 1819, pp.255–56.

147 *Newcastle Chronicle*, 7 July 1816, p.4.

148 Revd J. Black, *Presbyterianism in Sunderland and the North*, 1876, p.10.

149 R. Hyslop, *200 Years 1739–1939*, 1939, p.12 and plate.

150 *Sunderland Herald*, 13 August 1836, p.3; G.R. Potts, 'Methodist Chapels and the Gothic Revival', *Proceedings of the Wesley Historical Society*, May 1991, p.43; G.R. Potts, op. cit., 2007.

151 Corder Manuscripts.

152 Information from G.E. Milburn.

153   *Sunderland Herald*, 14 November 1851, p.5; *In Memoriam. Robert Whitaker McAll*, 1898, pp.12 and 15; *Builder*, 19 November 1853, p.705 and 3 December 1853, p.733.

154   See G.E. Milburn, *Church and Chapel in Sunderland, 1780–1914*, 1988, p.19.

155   *Sunderland Herald*, 9 June 1865, p.8.

156   *Sunderland Herald*, 31 May 1867, p.2.

157   G.R. Potts, op. cit., 2007.

158   G.R. Potts, op. cit., 2007.

159   G.R. Potts, op. cit., 2007. See Congregational, Sorley Street, 1891; Mount Tabor Methodist New Connexion,1894; Chester Rd; Roker Wesleyan, 1905.

160   *Sunderland Daily Echo*, 3 August 1880, pp.3–4 and 29 September 1881, p.3.

161   *Sunderland Times*, 7 April 1874, p.3 and 31 August 1875, p.3; G.E. Milburn, 'Tensions in Primitive Methodism in the Eighteen Seventies and the Origins of the Christian Lay Churches in the North East', *Proceedings of the Wesley Historical Society*, February 1976, pp.93–101 and 135–45.

162   *Sunderland Daily Echo*, 20 April 1881 and 26 January 1883, p.3; *Building News*, 45, 28 December 1883, p.1043.

163   G.E. Milburn, *Church and Chapel in Sunderland, 1780–1914*, 1988, p.22.

164   *Sunderland Times*, 20 May 1887.

165   *Sunderland Daily Echo*, 8 February 1884, p.3 and 6 February 1889, p.3.

166   *Sunderland Daily Echo*, 22 April 1891, p.3.

167   *Sunderland Daily Echo*, 6 May 1901, p.3.

168   *Sunderland Daily Echo*, 28 August 1902, p.3; *Sunderland Year Book*, 1906, p.124 and plate.

169   Anon., *Ewesley Road Methodist Church 75ᵀᴴ Anniversary*, 1979.

170   *Sunderland Daily Echo*, 3 August 1891, p.3.

171   *Builder*, 99, 1 October 1910, p.361; *Sunderland Daily Echo*, 6 October 1910.

172   *Sunderland Daily Echo*, 28 May 1888, p.4; G.E. Milburn (ed.), *St John's Ashbrooke: a church and its story 1888–1988*, 1988.

173   *Sunderland Daily Echo*, 22 February 1887, p.3.

174   J. Sykes, *Local Records*, 1866, pp.250 and 280; *Sunderland Herald*, 27 September 1834, p.2.

175   *Sunderland Daily Echo*, 4 November 1880, p.3.

176   It was built on the site of the house owned by Dr William Reid Clanny (1776–1850), a founding member of the Subscription Library.

177   *Sunderland Herald*, 25 January 1850; *Building News*, 75, 16 December 1898, p.xiii.

178   *Sunderland Herald*, 25 January 1850.

179   *Sunderland Daily Echo*, 20 December 1887, p.3.

180   *Sunderland Times*, 17 December 1875, p.8.

181   *Sunderland Times*, 17 December 1875, p.8; *Sunderland Daily Echo*, 22 April 1878, pp.2–3.

182   *Kelly's Directory*, 1894, p.361.

183   *Building News*, 10 February 1871, p.104.

184   *Builder*, 37, 1879, p.1379 and plate; I.S. Black, 'National Provincial Bank Building in North-East England in the later Nineteenth Century', *Durham Archaeological Journal*, 17, 2003, pp.63–82 and plates.

185   See I.S. Black, op. cit., 2003, pp.63–82.

186   *Sunderland Daily Echo*, 30 January 1891, p.3; Obituary of Gribble, *Building News*, 68, 29 March 1895, p.440.

187   *Sunderland Daily Echo*, 2 June 1902, p.5 and 10 May 1905, p.3.

188   *Sunderland Times*, 10 July 1874, p.8; G.R. Potts, op. cit., 2007; Sketchbook, photocopy in Sunderland Museum.

189   F. Caws, 'Concrete Floors', *RIBA Journal*, 7, 1899, pp.189–97.

190   *Sunderland Daily Echo*, 19 December 1879, p.3 and 18 August 1880, pp.2–3.

191 *Sunderland Daily Echo*, 19 December 1879, p.3 and 3 December 1880, p.3.

192 *Sunderland Daily Echo*, 15 July 1885, p.3 and 16 October 1885, p.3.

193 *Building News*, 3 October 1890, p.489.

194 *Sunderland Daily Echo*, 24 September 1890, p.2.

195 At the first general meeting of the Association Caws gave a paper entitled 'The Study of Mechanics in their Relation to Architecture.' *Building News*, 14 March 1890, p.397.

196 D.J. Blair, *The Spatial Dynamics of Commercial Activity in Central Sunderland*, unpublished MA dissertation, Durham University, 1977.

197 *Sunderland Daily Echo*, 16 March 1882, p.2.

198 *Sunderland Daily Echo*, 10 November 1886, p.2.

199 *Sunderland Daily Echo*, 2 March 1905, p.5.

200 *Sunderland Daily Echo*, 23 March 1885, p.4 and 1 October 1887, p.3.

201 *Sunderland Daily Echo*, 27 April 1889, p.3; P. Gibson, *History of Southwick*, 1986, p.9 and plate.

202 Corder Manuscripts, *Bishopwearmouth, vol. 1*, pp.149–57.

203 TWAS, DT.TRM/5/53–115.

204 *Kelly's Directory*, 1894, p.361.

205 *Building News*, 17 September 1869, p.221.

206 W.H. Hoskins appears to have worked in partnership with his brother and took over the practice when George retired in 1907. See *Builder*, 29 April 1921, p.544; *Darlington and Stockton Times*, 23 April 1921, p.3.

207 *Building News*, 81, 7 September 1901, p.436; *Who's Who in Architecture*, 1914.

208 *Sunderland Daily Echo*, 13 October 1881, p.2; *Architect*, 25, 16 April 1881, p.53.

209 *Building News*, 54, 18 May 1888, p.720.

210 M. Girouard, *Victorian Pubs*, 1984; L.F. Pearson, *The Northumbrian Pub*, 1989.

211 L.F. Pearson, op. cit., 1989, pp.122 and 98; TWAS, 234/485, 1–55; P Gibson, op. cit., 1986, p.8.

212 L.F. Pearson, op. cit., 1989, p.137; Sunderland Museum, Drawings; *Building News*, 79, 21 December 1900, p.900.

213 Department of Environment, *Listed Buildings Record*, p32; P Gibson, op. cit., 1986, p.8 and plate.

214 *Building News*, 83, 12 September 1902, pp.363–64 and plate; LF Pearson, op. cit., 1989, pp.85–86.

215 TWAS, DT.TRM/2/157–160; LF Pearson, op. cit., 1989, pp.81–82, 126 and plates.

216 E. Watts Moses, *To Ashbrooke and Beyond: The History of Sunderland Cricket and Rugby Football Club 1808–1963*, 1963, p.27.

217 *Building News*, 74, 24 June 1898, pp.885–86.

218 S. Inglis, *Engineering Archie: Archibald Leitch – football ground designer*, 2005, pp.124–27.

219 *Sunderland Herald*, 28 February, 1840, p.2; *Sunderland Times*, 7 October 1871, p.5.

220 *Sunderland Herald*, 4 January 1856, p.7.

221 *Sunderland Herald*, 27 August 1852, p.5; 24 August 1855, p.5; 14 September 1855, p.5. *Old Sunderland*, 1977, p25. *Monthly Chronicle*, February 1891, pp.86–87. *Sunderland Year Book*, 1906, pp.17–19.

222 *Sunderland Daily Echo*, 24 October 1882, p.2.

223 *Sunderland Daily Echo*, 3 August 1891, p.2; A. Pickersgill, *Sunderland in Times Past*, 1981, plate.

224 *Sunderland Daily Echo*, 24 March 1906, p.3; *Builder*, 91, 12 January 1907, p.32. L.F. Pearson, 'The Architecture of Entertainment Run Riot: William Hope of Newcastle, 1862–1907', *Northern History*, 27, 1991, pp.184–97.

225 *Sunderland Daily Echo*, 27 June 1907, p.5; *Builder*, 93, July 1907, p.88.

226 G.R. Potts, op. cit., 2007; I. Mackintosh and M. Sell (eds), *Curtains!!!, or a New Life for Old Theatres*, 1982, p.214.

227 A. Anderson, *The Dream Palaces of Sunderland*, 1982, pp.20–23.

228 *Sunderland Daily Echo*, 23 December 1912, p.8; 30 April 1912, p.2; 19 December 1913, p.3; 18 November 1913, p.5.

229 *Sunderland Daily Echo*, 10 December 1915, p.7; A. Anderson, op. cit., 1982, pp.52–55.

230 *Who's Who in Architecture*, 1914, p.212; A. Anderson, op. cit., 1982, pp.44–45.

231 DCRO, Q/D/P/43; T. Corfe (ed.), op. cit., 1983, p.18.

232 Sunderland Museum, Drawing TWCMS: C11848.

233 J. Murray, 'Account of the removal of the Light-house at Sunderland', *Proceedings of the Institution of Civil Engineers*, 3, 1844, pp.342–55. Obituary of Murray, *Proceedings of the ICE*, 71, 1883, pp.400–07.

234 DCRO, Q/P/D/123; 156; 213; 233; J. Murray, 'On the Progressive Construction of the Sunderland Docks', *Proc. ICE*, 15, 1855–56, pp.418–55.

235 Obituary of Meik in *Proceedings of the ICE*, 125, 1896, pp.410–12; Entry for Sir William Halcrow in *Oxford DNB. Online*, 2004.

236 N.T. Sinclair, *The River Wear*, 1984, p.11 and plate.

237 *Sunderland Daily Echo*, 17 February 1911, p.5.

238 Another Customs Office was built in Tatham Street in 1907 by H.N. Hawkes of the Office of Works, *Sunderland Daily Echo*, 16 May 1907.

239 *Builder*, 87, 17 September 1904 and 98, 18 June 1910, p.696 and plates; Quotation from *Sunderland Year Book*, 1907, p.113.

240 N. Pevsner and E. Williamson, op. cit., 1983, p.468.

241 W. Fordyce, *Durham II*, 1857, p.522.

242 *Sunderland Herald and Times*, 28 August 1869.

243 G. Woodward, 'Trubshaw, Hartley and Harrison: early nineteenth century engineers and architects', *Transactions of the Newcomen Society*, 2001, pp.72 and 77.

244 N.T. Sinclair, *The River Wear*, 1984, p.46 and plate.

245 *Transport Heritage* website, accessed 7 June 2011.

246 T. Corfe (ed.), op. cit., 1983, p.19.

247 G. Woodward, op. cit.

248 Information from John Tumman.

249 B. Fawcett, *History of NER Architecture, vol. 3: Bell and Beyond*, NERA, 2005, pp.9–14 and plates.

250 B. Fawcett, op. cit., 2005, pp.116 and 166 and plate.

251 F.C. Buscarlet and A. Hunter, 'The Queen Alexandra Bridge over the River Wear, Sunderland', *Proceedings of the ICE*, 182, 1909–10, pp.59–93.

252 DCRO, Q/D/P/342; 348; 364.

253 S.A. Staddon, *The Tramways of Sunderland*, 1964, pp.11–21.

254 *Building News*, 19 October 1900, p.539.

255 'Sunderland Corporation Electricity Works, *The Electrician*, 5 September 1902, pp.779–84; *Sunderland Daily Echo*, 2 February 1904, p.5; DCRO, Q/D/P/436, 499, 526. Entry for Sir John Snell, *Oxford DNB Online*, 2004.

256 *Sunderland Daily Echo*, 20 April 1905, p.6; *Builder*, 88, 29 April 1903.

257 *Sunderland Daily Echo*, 30 September 1903, p.6; 20 April 1905, p.6; *Builder*, 88, 29 April 1903; G.R. Potts, op. cit., 2007.

258 The Little Egypt estate was so called because it incorporated Cairo Street and Tel El Kebir Road.

259 G.E. Milburn and S.T. Miller, op. cit., 1988, p.222 gives fuller figures.

260 *Pigot's Directory*, 1822; *Ward's Directory*,1900.

261 *Pigot's Directory*, 1822; *Kelly's Directory*, 1902.

262 Corder Manuscripts, *Bishopwearmouth*, 1, pp.149–57; R. Hyslop, 'The Fawcett Estate', *Antiquities of Sunderland*, XIX, 1929–32, pp.29–41.

263 N. Pevsner, *Buildings of England: County Durham*, 1953, pp.229–30. Corrected in second edition of 1983.

264 Corder Manuscripts, *Family Pedigrees*, 4, pp.343–45.

265 Two Houses in Frederick Street by Potts, *Sunderland Herald*, 7 April 1843, p1; House in Fawcett Street by Pratt, *Sunderland Herald*, 25 July 1845, p.1; House in John Street by Middlemiss, *Sunderland Herald*, 28 June 1850, p.1.

266 Sunderland Corporation, Deed Packet 803. These deeds are not all currently in Corporation hands.

267 *Sunderland Herald*, 9 April 1841, p.1.

268 H.M. Colvin, op. cit., 1995, pp.427–30.

269 Sunderland Corporation, Deed Packet 128.

270 Plan, Tyne and Wear County Museums Service, B10184; *Sunderland Herald*, 23 September 1853, p.4; 3 June 1853, p.4; TWAS, SDB/A6/1/1, pp.47 and 63; *Sunderland Daily Echo*, 26 May 1884, p.2.

271 Minutes of Sunderland Borough Sanitary Committee, TWAS, SDB/A6/1/1; CL. Cummings, 'Some Account of St George's Square and the People Connected Therewith', *Antiquities of Sunderland*, 7, 1906, pp.53–80.

272 TWAS, SDB/A6/1/1.

273 Estate plan, Ryhope Lane/Tunstall Road, *Sunderland Herald*, 17 September 1852, p.4; Plans for Villas, *Sunderland Herald*, 22 October 1852, p.4. Estate plan, Ryhope Road, *Sunderland Herald*, 31 August 1855, p.4; *Building News*, 3, 18 September 1857, p.991.

274 *Sunderland Daily Echo*, 4 September 1884, p.4 and 4 February 1896, p.3.

275 Photograph in Sunderland Museum Collection.

276 Sunderland Corporation, Deed Packet 9737; *Newcastle Daily Journal*, 16 January 1865; *Newcastle Chronicle*, 1 January 1887; T. Faulkner and A Greg, *John Dobson: Architect of the North East*, 2001, p.178.

277 Sunderland Corporation, Deed Packet 916; W. Scarff, *Durham in the Twentieth Century*, 1906, photo p.74.

278 F. Caws, FRIBA Nomination Papers, 1893; *Sunderland Post*, 20 December 1887, p.3.

279 Auction details, *Sunderland Daily Echo*, 18 May 1876, p.3; Greener's plan, *Sunderland Daily Echo*, 27 July 1876, p.1; *Builder*, 40, 29 January 1881, p.124 and plate.

280 John Tillman, FRIBA Nomination Papers, 1887; *Sunderland Daily Echo*, 13 April 1905, p.4.

281 M. Girouard, *Sweetness and Light*, 1977, p.1.

282 J.J. Stevenson, *House Architecture*, 1880, p.17.

283 Sunderland Corporation, Deed Packet 61; T. Corfe, *Langham Tower*, Sunderland Polytechnic Booklet, n.d.

284 *Sunderland Herald*, 10 April 1840, p.1 and 18 June 1841, p.3.

285 *Sunderland Times*, 10 August 1869, p.5; 14 August 1869, p.2.

286 *Sunderland Daily Echo*, 23 June 1880, pp.2–3.

287 *Sunderland Daily Echo*, 23 June 1884, p.2.

288 *Building News*, 80, 31 August 1901, p.749; *Sunderland Daily Echo*, 10 April 1905, p.3.

289 Information from J. Gould, architect in the firm of G.T. Brown and Son.

290 *Builder*, 19, 2 February 1861, p.81; 20 April 1861, p.274.

291 See A. Long, 'The Sunderland Cottage' in T.E. Faulkner (ed.), *Northumbrian Panorama*, 1996, pp.97–122.

292 E.A. Longstaffe, *New Housing in Sunderland c.1860–1870*, unpublished BA Dissertation, Sunderland Polytechnic, 1982.

293 M.J. Daunton, *House and Home in the Victorian City: Working Class Housing, 1850–1914*, 1983, pp.197–98; Longstaffe, op. cit., 1982.

294 *Sunderland Herald*, 7 April 1865, p.8.

295 *Sunderland Herald*, 14 August 1857, p.4.

296 *Sunderland Daily Echo*, 26 August 1879, p.3; 26 May 1884, p.2.

297 Long, op. cit., 1996, p.98. However, Long does demonstrate that some of the later cottages were designed by W. and T.R. Milburn.

298 See Johnson, M., 'The Sunderland Cottage: Evolution of a Housing Type', unpublished report for Durham VCH and Johnson, M., 'The Sunderland Cottage: "The favourite and typical dwelling of the skilled mechanic"' in *Vernacular Architecture*, vol. 41, 2010, pp.59–74.

299 See TWAS, 269/2180, a plan of nine cottages in Forfar Street for C.B. Carr, dated 14 April 1926. See also TWAS, 269/3587, a plan of seven cottages in Inverness Street for Rackstraw and Thompson, dated 10 October 1923.

300 See TWAS, 269/3587, a plan of seven cottages in Inverness Street for Rackstraw and Thompson, dated 10 October 1923.

301 See TWAS, 269/4087, a plan of 21 cottages in Mafeking Street for J.W. White, dated 18 July 1924.

302 See TWAS, 269/5918, a plan of six cottages in St Leonard's Street, dated 13 February 1924.

303 *Building News*, 88, 7 April 1905, p.516; 19 May 1905, p.735.

304 T.E. Faulkner and A. Greg, op. cit., 2001, p.170.

305 W. Fordyce, *Durham II*, 1857, p.480; T.E. Faulkner and A. Greg, op. cit., 2001, p.111; Monkwearmouth Local History Group, *More Monkwearmouth Memories*, 1990, p.27 for photo of Victor Street (formerly Ann Street). Quotation from Fordyce.

306 Estate Plan in Sunderland Museum.

307 *Building News*, 22, 16 February 1872, p.139; D.H. Tasker, *Housing and Public Health in Victorian Sunderland c.1840–1905*, unpublished BA dissertation, Hull University, 1986, p.50.

308 *Sunderland Daily Echo*, 2 June 1896, p.3.

309 Sunderland Borough General Improvement Committee Minutes, TWAS, SDB/A9/1/1–13; *Sunderland Times*, 9 July 1870, p.2 and 5; 7 February 1871, p.2.

310 D.H. Tasker, op. cit., 1986, p.51.

311 G. Patterson, 'Harrison's Buildings – Sunderland's First Council Housing', *Sunderland's History*, 3, 1985, pp.5–34.

312 *Sunderland Times*, 3 November 1874, p.3.

313 *Sunderland Daily Echo*, 21 May 1909, p.3 and photo.

Index